SHADY BUSINESS

Irwin Ross

SHADY BUSINESS

CONFRONTING CORPORATE CORRUPTION

The Twentieth Century Fund Press

The Twentieth Century Fund is a research foundation undertaking timely analyses of economic, political, and social issues. Not-for-profit and non-partisan, the Fund was founded in 1919 and endowed by Edward A. Filene.

HV
6769
R67
1992

Library of Congress Cataloging-in-Publication Data

Ross, Irwin, 1919–
    Shady business : confronting corporate corruption / Irwin Ross.
        p. cm.
    Includes index and bibliographic references.
    ISBN 0-87078-340-8 : $19.95. — ISBN 0-87078-341-6 (pbk.) : $9.95
    1. Corporations—United States—Corrupt practices. I. Title.
HV6769.R67 1992
364.1'68'0973—dc20   92-29437
                                                              CIP

Cover Design and Illustration: Claude Goodwin
Manufactured in the United States of America.
Copyright © 1992 by the Twentieth Century Fund, Inc.

For my wife, Patricia

FOREWORD

In the 1980s we heard, "greed is good." We were told that greed lubricates the engines of capitalism. Each of us pursuing our own economic interest helps to create a society in which all of us are better off. Better off meaning, in this case, that we have more money, more goods, more of what we want. And all because we said yes to that impulse to want more in the first place. It is an idea almost elegant in its simplicity.

But in the 1990s we have discovered that religious faith in capitalism alone would not make all of us, after all, better off. We have been reminded of the need to set limits on where our pursuit of self-interest might take us. We create rules: zoning regulations, liquor licenses, securities laws, and fiduciary responsibilities. We rely upon a web of limits and obligations designed to control the consequences of unbridled greed.

In other words, we recognize that in reaching for that little extra for ourselves or our companies we benefit from a certain restraint, some of it backed by the threat of sanctions. In this sense we know our limits; we know we are capable of venality and even have a weakness for it. Yet we remain surprised at the frequency with which we give in to this particular temptation. Big companies and small, con men, and billionaires all too often stretch the limits we have set on just how much greed is in fact good.

In the last few years the reporting and literature about American business has featured a wealth of material focused on the evils of greed. Here at the Twentieth Century Fund, fairly early in this national reassessment, we supported an important contribution to the field, John Brooks's *The Takeover Game*. Much earlier the Fund supported an examination of *Corporate Control, Corporate Power* by Edward S. Herman and *Who Owns the Corporation? Management vs. Shareholders* by Edward Jay Epstein.

In this sense, this book by Irwin Ross, a noted journalist, extends a long Twentieth Century Fund tradition of exploration into the central issues raised by interplay of capitalism, democracy, and the public interest. We are pleased to publish this book as the first clothbound volume under the Twentieth Century Fund Press imprint.

Richard C. Leone, *President*
The Twentieth Century Fund
August 1992

ACKNOWLEDGMENTS

I am grateful to a number of people for sharing their ideas about the subjects canvassed in this volume or for answering endless questions about the cases and situations in which they were professionally involved. I thank Stanley Arkin, Joseph J. Aronica, Bruce Drucker, Gary Edwards, Wilson Fadely, William F. Fahey, John Fleder, Jonny J. Frank, Jacqueline Frend, John Fricano, Rudolph Giuliani, Joseph A. Grundfest, Fred D. Heather, Henry E. Hudson, Linda Imes, Harold E. Kohn, Robert I. Jacobs, Bruce Kovens, Gary Lynch, William McLucas, Bruce V. Milburn, Inar Morics, Jay Rakoff, Herbert Robinson, Charles Rule, David Spears, Gordon Spivack, John Sturc, Thomas Roche, Joseph H. Widmar, Alan R. Yuspeh.

I am also indebted to Daniel Seligman, who read the entire manuscript and made many acute observations; to Hays Gorey, Jr., David Jordan, Paul F. Math, and John S. Siffert, who read portions of the manuscript and steered me away from some embarrassing errors; to Abdulkadir Haireche for imaginative assistance in locating research materials; to my wife, Patricia Brooke Ross, who handled a number of research assignments with her customary efficiency and aplomb; to my friend and lawyer Nancy Wechsler, who provided valuable assistance and advice at many points in the gestation and development of this project. At the Twentieth Century Fund, which supported the book, I was greatly helped by the shrewd counsel of John Samples, the editorial skills of Beverly Goldberg, and the sharp eye and deft pencil of Steven Greenfield, who did the copyediting. I thank them all as well.

CONTENTS

CHAPTER 1

THE ENIGMA OF CORPORATE CRIME

There is no lack of variety, ingenuity and daring in corporate crime. Anyone who doubts this has only to recall the scandals associated with the names of Michael Milken, Ivan Boesky, Leona Helmsley, Salomon Brothers—or any number of large defense contractors. For example:

▲ In October 1988, the Sundstrand Corporation of Rockford, Illinois, agreed to plead guilty to four criminal counts and to pay the U.S. Treasury $115 million—by far the largest penalty to be imposed up to that time in a case of defense procurement fraud.

The fraud had been spectacular in its brazenness. Sundstrand, which manufactures aerospace parts, had persistently submitted unrealistically low bids to secure contracts, then recouped its excess costs by fraudulently allocating them to overhead accounts that the Defense Department paid for separately. In addition, the company took phony tax losses, gave gratuities to procurement officials, and billed the government for millions of dollars in spurious charges that disguised such curious items as saunas, movies, golf expenses, household servants.[1]

▲ The investment firm of Salomon Brothers, hitherto untouched by the scandals that had roiled Wall Street, shocked the financial world in August 1991 by admitting that it had blatantly violated the rules of government bond auctions. From time to time, Salomon had disguised some of its bids as those of customers to enable the firm to garner more than the 35 percent share of the securities at auction to which all bidders were limited. The

1

purpose of the Treasury rule, of course, was to prevent one or two bidders from cornering the market in an issue and putting the squeeze on other traders. In one instance, it was later discovered, Salomon had gobbled up 61 percent of a new Treasury issue. One revelation followed another after the scandal broke, and in a matter of days the top officials of the firm felt compelled to resign. In May 1992, a chastened, reformed and slimmed-down Salomon agreed to put up $290 million to settle all charges; $190 million were fines and penalties and $100 million represented a fund to pay civil claims.

▲ Early in 1991, Michael Milken, the self-made billionaire who created the "junk bond" craze of the 1980s, began a ten-year prison sentence that followed his guilty plea to six felony counts involving violations of the securities and tax laws. It was an extraordinary end to a flamboyant career and was the final act (the collapse of Milken's firm, Drexel Burnham Lambert, was the penultimate one) in a bizarre scenario that began more modestly with the sudden unmasking of Dennis B. Levine in 1986. Levine was a young, swift-rising mergers and acquisitions specialist at Drexel who earned $12.4 million on the side in illegal securities trades based on inside information, much of it fed to him by a network of tipsters. He shielded his operation for years by dealing through foreign banks, and it was only by sheer chance that he was eventually exposed. When the case broke, the size of Levine's loot made him the biggest insider trader to be caught by the Securities and Exchange Commission. But he was only the first. Rather than fight the charges, Levine cooperated with the authorities to mitigate his sentence (he received a two-year prison term) and named a number of coconspirators.

The most startling was Ivan Boesky, the best-known arbitrageur on Wall Street, a man who had built an awesome reputation for shrewdness, daring and great tactical skill. Boesky's entire business was arbitrage; he had a huge following of institutional and wealthy individual investors who funded him with $500 million in speculative capital. Now Boesky's genius was suddenly revealed to involve little more than the deft exploitation of inside information.

The penalty he paid became the biggest for insider trading or other securities fraud up to that date—$100 million, half of which was a fine and the other half a fund against which defrauded investors could make claims. Boesky also cooperated with the government (receiving a relatively modest three-year prison term), and among the names he offered up were Milken and Martin A. Siegel, formerly of Kidder, Peabody and recently of Drexel Burnham Lambert.

Siegel was a star and a golden boy, a whiz at mergers and acquisitions who had been one of the top performers at Kidder. He was also, it soon became clear, a brilliant manipulator of inside information whose transgressions had benefited both Kidder and himself. He pled guilty, parted with $9 million to settle with the SEC, and while awaiting sentencing followed Levine's and Boesky's examples in naming names. He finally received a sentence of only two months in prison. Milken, a much bigger catch who did not cooperate with the government until after his sentencing, was treated more severely than almost anyone anticipated.[2]

▲ In August 1988, the Hertz Rent a Car company, the country's largest, pled guilty to charges of defrauding customers by inflating repair bills. Hertz paid a $6.85 million fine—touted as the largest ever in a consumer fraud case—and established a $13.7 million fund for restitution to victimized customers or their insurance companies. The scam was shameless: in some cases, Hertz charged for repair work that had not even been performed, producing counterfeit invoices. Some 110,000 customers (or their insurers) were out of pocket. Had a disaffected employee in Hertz's Boston office not blown the whistle, the fraud might still be going on.[3]

▲ From 1978 through 1986, three enterprising New Yorkers enriched themselves through an ingenious tax-dodging scheme in Manhattan's garment center. The trio set up more than thirty-six shell corporations that did no business apart from selling phony invoices to companies seeking to reduce their tax liabilities. These companies would pay the invoices by check and receive back, in cash, 85 to 95 percent of their remittances, the difference being the invoice sellers' commissions. The invoice purchasers entered the full value of the checks on their books as expense items, thereby reducing their profits and hence their tax bills. Over the years, according to the government, more than $136 million in phony invoices had been sold to some two hundred companies. The invoice sellers were convicted and sentenced to prison terms ranging from four months to three years.[4]

The foregoing are typical recent examples of corporate crime—defined as crime that benefits the corporation, whose purpose is to enhance corporate profits. This book is not concerned with the sort of crime that victimizes the corporation (such as employee theft, self-dealing, embezzlement). Anyone reading the financial pages knows that corporate crime as here defined is frequently dramatic and sometimes startling in its audacity and arrogance. It is also a perplexing phenomenon, for the offenders include some of the most prominent and respected corporations in the land, and the employees who do the actual dirty work are usually otherwise upright, law-abiding citizens. They have nothing in common with embezzlers or professional con men who move from town to town and from scam to scam, constituting a demimonde as remote from the life of the average businessperson as the Mafia types who run shakedown rackets or traffic in drugs.

But not at all remote from the workaday world of industry and commerce are businessmen who engage in price-fixing or bid rigging, salesmen who pay kickbacks to purchasing agents, defense contractors who inflate bills submitted to the Pentagon, or small merchants who "skim" money from cash registers to cheat the tax collector, not to speak of middle managers at a leading auto manufacturer who a few years ago ordered that odometers on used cars be turned back before the cars were sold as new. None of these people think of themselves as criminals, for they tend to view their illegal acts as victimless crimes from which they do not personally benefit (except insofar as a good job performance may ultimately bring its rewards). Nor, indeed, are these individuals criminals in the sense of being devoted to a life of crime on a full-time basis. Their criminality is intermittent and strictly an adjunct to their legitimate pursuits. If caught, they tend to view themselves as victims of an inequitable system.

Corporate crime is hardly new. Yet, despite the headlines, the phenomenon tends to be minimized in any catalog of social ills. In part this is because more traditional forms of crime—street crime, racketeering, drug trafficking—pose far more serious threats. Moreover, corporate corruption is mistakenly regarded as an aberration, the result of a "bad apple" or two in the corporate barrel, rather than a frequent occurrence in some companies and some types of economic activity. Criminal behavior is not an inevitable feature of corporate life, but it is certainly a standing temptation to which companies often succumb. In the case of price-fixing, Adam Smith took a more mordant view in a famous passage in *The Wealth of Nations*: "People of the same trade seldom meet together, even for merriment and diversion, but the conversation ends in a conspiracy against the public, or in some contrivance to raise prices."[5]

Corporate corruption thrives because efforts to repress it are ineffective and sporadic. It receives inadequate attention from law enforcement agencies, whose resources are always stretched thin, and it is often viewed with indifference by top corporate management until a scandal focuses attention. Frequently, it is only after a corporation is hit by a large criminal antitrust action that top management starts a compliance program to educate middle management. To be sure, one or another aspect of corporate crime periodically becomes the target of a well-publicized cleanup campaign. Insider trading became such a target on the part of the SEC and the U.S. attorney in Manhattan, starting in the middle 1980s. During the 1970s, foreign bribery and illegal political contributions by corporations received great attention, having come to light by chance in the wake of the Watergate investigation. But overall enforcement of the relevant laws is always spotty.

Corporate crime deserves far more attention, if only because of the economic toll that it exacts. Gaining significant business advantage through bribery or price-fixing at the very least diminishes economic efficiency and, at worst, may destroy it in particular sectors. Beyond that, business corruption, like political corruption, can have a demoralizing impact on organizations in which it is rife, not to speak of the community at large, promoting a sense that only the tricksters and cheats win the big prizes.

For its immediate victims, corporate crime imposes sizable costs, which can often be quantified. The whole purpose of price-fixing, for example, is to exact a higher price from customers than would be set by competition. The precise amount of that differential is argued in a class action lawsuit (following a criminal conviction), in which the victimized customers try to recoup their losses and to claim the triple damages that the law allows. Frequently, the suit is settled before trial, and the compromise sum can be taken as a rough (probably conservative) guide to the economic burden of the price-fixing scheme. In 1983, for example, a lengthy lawsuit in the celebrated corrugated box case was finally settled with the plaintiffs receiving $550 million; the largest consumer among the plaintiffs got $15 million. Hardly trifling sums, and that case was but one of many.

To take another field, the economic burden of kickbacks can often be gauged by the sums of money the seller passes to the purchasing agent, for the bribes are generally tacked on to the sales price. (It is possible, of course, that a kickback can come out of a seller's profit, but this is less common.) In imposing sentence in a kickback case, the judge on occasion orders restitution to the victimized company of the money its buyer received.

In insider trading cases, the profit earned by the illegal trader would otherwise accrue to shareholders not in possession of the inside information. There is a finite amount of profit (or loss) between any two prices at which a security trades. If part of that profit is appropriated by someone acting on inside information, it is obviously lost to others who trade the stock. That forgone profit is the economic cost of the offense—a cost sustained by those cheated. In the Boesky case, the $50 million fund to make victims whole is some measure of the magnitude of his thefts.

In tax evasion cases, the U.S. Treasury obviously bears the cost—the amount of unpaid taxes. In the invoice-selling case mentioned earlier, the government calculated that the total value of the invoices came to more than $136 million. To determine the IRS's loss, one would need to know the marginal tax rates of all the companies that participated in the scam. Assuming it was 20 percent on average, the Treasury lost $27.2 million.

How widespread is corporate crime? The answer depends partly on how the term is defined—what offenses are included; and partly on the statistical measures—does one count only convictions or civil court judgments as well, and perhaps even the rulings of administrative tribunals? Are allegations statistically meaningful? There is no agreement on these matters. The first of the few academic inquiries in this field, White Collar Crime, published in 1949 by the eminent sociologist Edwin

H. Sutherland, uses the term white-collar crime as a synonym for corporate crime, defining it "as a crime committed by a person of respectability and high social status in the course of his occupation." The last phrase is the operative one, for Sutherland excludes "many crimes of the upper class, such as most cases of murder, intoxication, or adultery since these are not a part of the occupational procedures."[6] Moreover, Sutherland clearly meant his term to apply only to crimes committed on behalf of the corporation, as is apparent from the list of offenses covered, among them restraint of trade, misrepresentation in advertising, copyright and patent infringement, unfair labor practices as determined by the National Labor Relations Board, financial fraud, violations of war regulations.

The heart of the book is an analysis of the records of seventy large nonfinancial corporations, culled from two lists of two hundred of the largest such corporations published in 1929 and 1938. Sutherland's researches covered the life span (averaging forty-five years) of each of his corporations, none of which did he name in the edition published in his lifetime. A corporation is cited as an offender as a result of any adverse decision, civil or criminal, by a court or an administrative commission.

On the basis of these criteria, the score was 980 adverse decisions for Sutherland's 70 corporations, with 14 the average per corporation and 50 the maximum—over the lifetime of any one corporation. The seriousness of the offenses varied greatly, with 60 corporations cited for restraint of trade, 53 for copyright, patent, or trademark infringement, 44 for unfair labor practices, 28 for advertising misrepresentation, 26 for illegal rebates, and 43 for miscellaneous delinquencies.[7]

In their 1980 book, *Corporate Crime*, Marshall B. Clinard and Peter C. Yeager defined their subject as "any act committed by corporations that is punished by the state, regardless of whether it is punished under administrative, civil or criminal law."[8] It was in essence the same definition as Sutherland's, but it covered many more federal agencies—twenty-five of them, ranging from the Agriculture Marketing Service to the Consumer Product Safety Commission to the Labor Deparment's wage and hour division, as well as the criminal, tax, and antitrust divisions of the Department of Justice. More agencies existed than in Sutherland's time, naturally.

The corporate universe surveyed consisted of 477 of the nation's largest publicly owned corporations as well as 105 of the biggest companies in the wholesale, retail, and service fields; the period covered was

1975 and 1976.[9] With a grant from the Law Enforcement Assistance Administration, Clinard supervised a team of researchers who spent two years compiling the enforcement record of the 582 corporations. These data provide the statistical core of the book.

Clinard and Yeager found a good deal of crime, as they defined it and as measured by allegations. For the two years covered, 350 corporations (60 percent) had actions initiated against them—a total of 1,553 cases, an average of 4.4 per accused company—while 232 companies faced no charges whatsoever. Of the 477 manufacturing companies in the study, 71 were charged with multiple environmental offenses, 61 with multiple "manufacturing" offenses (by which the authors meant such matters as violations of the regulations of the Consumer Product Safety Commission), 8 with multiple "financial" violations (such as bribery and illegal political contributions), 6 with multiple unfair trade practices. A relatively small number of manufacturing corporations—a mere 32—confronted 52 percent of the charges.[10]

All these figures, it is important to emphasize, refer solely to accusations, which obviously makes them an uncertain guide to the incidence of corporate crime. The authors' defense is that these statistics are similar to arrest records, which are used as one measure of more traditional crimes. The authors do provide statistics on sanctions—1,529 imposed on manufacturing companies in the two-year period—but because of delays in the enforcement process not all sanctions relate to actions initiated during the same period; no correlation of the two sets of figures is provided.[11] Moreover, some of these sanctions may have been reversed on appeal after the period ended. The earlier study by Sutherland did not have this drawback, for it covered decades in the life of each company and dealt only with adverse decisions and penalties.

Both the Sutherland and Clinard-Yeager volumes are useful in sketching what might be regarded as the furthest statistical reaches of corporate crime, but they cannot be used for comparative purposes because they include different categories of crime. They also suffer from the very breadth of their coverage. Offenses of greatly varying seriousness are grouped together. Thus, in the Clinard-Yeager category of unfair trade practices the authors include not only price-fixing and bid rigging but also false and misleading advertising and illegal mergers. Misleading advertising is a minor matter compared to price-fixing, and the Justice Department handles an allegation of illegal merger in a civil rather than criminal proceeding.

Lumping together all manner of administrative findings and sanctions with the results of civil lawsuits as well as criminal convictions gives a fuzzy dimension to the problem. The inevitable result is endless argument over what is criminal and what is not. A more fruitful approach would be to narrow the focus to illegal activity the criminal character of which is fixed in law. In this way, one could at least determine the dimensions of hard-core criminal behavior by corporations over a period of time. That was the method used in an article I published on corporate crime in *Fortune* in December 1980.[12] The statistics in the article were limited to five crimes: criminal antitrust violations, bribery (including kickbacks and illegal rebates), illegal political contributions, fraud, tax evasion. I excluded foreign bribery by American corporations—many such cases had come to light in the 1970s—to avoid arguments as to whether such bribes should be considered criminal. There was a widely held view at the time, which I did not share, that bribery abroad should be condoned as an inevitable concomitant of doing business in a number of countries, some in the third world, some not.

For a corporation to be cited on the lists of offenders accompanying the article, either a conviction was necessary or there had to be a consent decree, such as those entered into with the SEC, in which the company neither confirmed nor denied the commission of a criminal act but agreed not to commit it in the future. The period covered in the *Fortune* survey was almost eleven years—from the beginning of 1970 to the autumn of 1980. The universe consisted of the 1,043 companies that had appeared at one time or another during the period on *Fortune's* lists of the country's largest industrial (the famous 500) and nonindustrial corporations—a total of 800; from year to year there were some newcomers on the list and others that fell off.

The compilation, spread over three pages of the magazine, showed a surprisingly high incidence of the five offenses. A total of 117 companies— 11 percent of those surveyed—were cited by name, offense, date, disposition. Several of the companies had multiple listings, for there were 188 citations. Antitrust violations constituted the largest category, with 98 citations, followed by 28 cases of kickbacks, bribery or illegal rebates, 21 cases of illegal political contributions, 11 fraud cases, and 5 instances of tax evasion.

The fact that 11 percent of the nation's largest and most prestigious corporations suffered the disgrace of criminal conviction (or nearly the equivalent by way of consent decrees) was enough to jolt even a jaded observer of the business scene. Moreover, fifty executives employed by fifteen companies were packed off to jail. The companies cited were a roll call of corporate renown—from American Airlines (illegal political contributions) to Du Pont (fixing prices of dyes in 1974) to Firestone (illegal political contributions and tax evasion) to Gulf Oil (more illegal political contributions) to International Paper (three cases of price-fixing in different fields—in 1974 and 1976). Many of these corporations, to be sure, had reformed procedures, cashiered executives, and instituted compliance programs after they were brought to book.

In its September 6, 1982, issue, *U.S. News & World Report* made a similar analysis of the record of the twenty-five largest U.S. corporations on the basis of their SEC filings, in which public companies are obliged to report to stockholders all material facts bearing on their performance. In the period since 1976, seven of the companies reported convictions for such offenses as price-fixing, illegal political contributions, the provision of free trips to an IRS agent, violation of the National Gas Act, and environmental pollution.

The *Fortune* and *U.S. News* data are now a decade or so old, but there is no reason to believe that the criminal propensities of American corporations are substantially different today. What has changed is the mix of corporate offenses. Illegal political contributions are largely a thing of the past. Corporations no longer maintain huge political slush funds, which were often accumulated by laundering money abroad. The spate of prosecutions in the 1970s killed off these funds, and there was no need to revive them after corporate political action committees were legalized. Now a corporation can lawfully raise as much money for political purposes as its executives and employees care to donate. Decriminalization, in effect, solved the problem in this area.

At the same time, the 1980s produced a long string of defense contract fraud cases of which the Sundstrand caper was only one of the most flamboyant. Such offenses have doubtless gone on for a long time, but they received only intermittent attention until the Department of Defense's Office of Inspector General, early in 1982, established the Defense Criminal Investigative Service, a detective force with field offices around the country that spends much of its time on procurement fraud. Since then, there have been hundreds of convictions of fraud-prone suppliers, mostly of smaller firms but also of a number of the DOD's top hundred contractors. In 1981, contractor abuses resulted in 151 suspensions and debarments—which meant that offending companies could no longer receive new defense contracts. In 1989, the DOD issued 1,179 such orders.[13]

There has also been an enormous upsurge in insider trading cases in recent years—largely as a result of the frenzy of hostile corporate takeovers, leveraged buy-outs and other merger activity in the 1980s. Cases are still coming to light that originated years ago. While insider trading has always existed, the profits it can generate while a merger is in prospect are spectacularly greater than those that could be realized from a tip on a favorable corporate development. When I was preparing the *Fortune* article, there was no need for a separate category for insider trading. Today one can hardly leave it out of a study of corporate crime, for it has enriched securities firms—Kidder, Peabody for example—as well as individual traders like Martin Siegel. Boesky's operation profited his company, while Levine only benefited himself.

The field of criminal antitrust is another in which violations continue with undiminished zeal; the past decade has seen an increase in the caseload of the antitrust division of the Justice Department. Typically, when the division ventures into a new field (having fortuitously received a promising lead), if it succeeds in making one case it is likely to end up with a treasure trove of cases, one leading to another. This occurred most dramatically in the electrical construction industry, as is related in detail in Chapter 3. In 1982, an anonymous letter to the chief of the antitrust division made a number of specific complaints of bid rigging in the industry, involving projects to build electrical generating plants, both nuclear and otherwise. An investigation was launched, and scores of cases were prosecuted. There have been some acquittals, but the antitrust division in the end won convictions against dozens of contractors—including most of the large companies in the industry at the time of the original complaint.

Several years earlier, the antitrust division received tips of bid-rigging rings in asphalt road construction in Virginia and Tennessee. These seemed to be local cases. The division investigated and won convictions. Most every case that was made generated information about bid-rigging activity in other localities; the cases continue to this day, with convictions in twenty-five states.[14] Results of this sort, originating from unsolicited tips, suggest that a lot of price-fixing exists in sectors into which the antitrust division has not had occasion to look.

While the mix of corporate crime has changed in recent years, there is no reason to believe that the overall situation is worse. The "decade of greed" has become the fashionable tag for the 1980s; the Reagan years are perceived to have been a period of egregious self-interest, which led to an enormous enrichment of the already rich, an excess of private and public debt, and a degree of conspicuous consumption that would have made Veblen feel quite at home. All this is true, yet the impact on corporate crime was largely limited to the financial area. Wall Street had its greatest boom ever, with excesses that in their outrageousness resembled those of the 1920s, though the degree of manipulation never rivaled the earlier era, owing to half a century of SEC regulation.

This book is an attempt to analyze the causes of corporate crime, the reasons it flourishes in some areas of the economy and not in others, the motives of its perpetrators, the rationales offered in its defense, the techniques used to detect it, and what further steps might be taken by both the public authorities and concerned corporations to repress it. It deals at length with six major areas of corporate crime: kickbacks and bribery; insider trading and associated securities violations; criminal antitrust activity; tax evasion; fraud in general; and fraud in defense procurement. No effort was made to be encyclopedic—environmental crime, for example, was not covered, nor was money laundering—for there was no need to deal with every variety of corporate crime in order to evaluate the phenomenon and advance some modest proposals to curb it.

The savings and loan crisis, replete with flamboyant and noisome examples of fraud and itself the subject of several books, was excluded for another reason: these frauds were not designed to profit the thrift institutions but to exploit them. Top executives enriched themselves through self-dealing, high living, and lavish compensation schemes, all to the detriment of their institutions, many of which ultimately went broke. The shareholders typically lost everything. Bank fraud as practiced by the rogue S&L's can be viewed as akin to embezzlement and is thus outside the scope of a book about the kind of criminal behavior that is advantageous to corporations.

We have horrors enough to deal with. A glance at history, to which the next chapter is devoted, may provide some perspective about our present circumstances. In many ways, we are better off than our fathers and grandfathers, who witnessed an exuberant degree of corporate brig-andage almost unfettered by the police power of the state. The legal power is now in place, but unless it is effectively used we are encourag-ing a dangerous degree of recidivism. For any study of the history of corporate crime suggests that the temptation is as elemental and deep-rooted as the profit motive itself.

CHAPTER 2

THE REPROBATE PAST

How does corporate corruption today compare with the past? Comparisons are useful, the better to understand the dynamics of the problem. Unfortunately, a statistical comparison is not possible, for there are no data for earlier decades similar to the figures Edwin Sutherland collected in the 1940s or that Marshall Clinard or *Fortune* compiled for the 1970s. Yet, despite the absence of statistics, a good deal of historical detail is available. Most of the evidence supports the conclusion that corporate conduct today, though nominally much improved over the past, is not at all superior when measured by present-day ethical standards.

Business crime today is rarely as blatant and is hardly as pervasive as in the post–Civil War era of the robber barons or in the manic years of the 1920s stock market boom. On the other hand, the corporate delinquencies of the past, however outrageous, were not always perceived as criminal when they occurred. They often enjoyed de facto legality, for government made little or no effort to repress them even when they apparently violated the common law. Moreover, these transgressions were not even universally regarded as unethical, and rarely so by businessmen (except those victimized). Today, by contrast, both the common and the more exotic forms of corporate misbehavior have long been statutorily illegal, and are almost universally condemned as unethical (their perpetrators frequently dissenting). Judged by the shifting criteria of social acceptability, corporate criminality today is worse than in the past.

Nothing in the modern era, however, can rival the predatory tactics of the entrepreneurs, promoters and stock speculators who flourished in the post–Civil War period. Corporate insiders routinely exploited their positions for private gain: conflict of interest and self-dealing were epidemic. Deceptive practices flourished on the stock exchanges, with "bear raids" and "corners" common occurrences; these markets were largely "efficient" in their ability to fleece the unwary. Bribery of legislators and judges was a common feature of the drive for corporate aggrandizement. Indeed, when corporations fought for advantage, no stratagem was beyond the pale, however underhanded and however dubious its legality, provided it worked for a time.

Long after the events, some take a more tolerant view of the old scandals. The buccaneering of the nineteenth-century robber barons is sometimes regarded as an inevitable ingredient of building a continent's infrastructure and consolidating its industrial base. The unbridled capitalism of that era, burdened with no constraints of custom or law to interfere with the drive to maximize market share and profits, did in fact lead to great material progress, although it eventually touched off a countervailing mobilization of victims and reformers. These groups successfully pressed for remedial legislation that, when finally enforced, ended the reign of the robber barons. Whether this entire train of events was inevitable, given the compulsions of the age, is impossible to say. Certainly alternative scenarios might be imagined. And one can recognize the achievements of the era without justifying its excesses, a balance difficult at the time.

Excesses remain today, to put it mildly. Some are new and different, but many are the same as in the distant past—insider trading, stock manipulation, fraud, the same yen for taming competition and fixing prices. In the corporate raids and protracted takeover battles of the 1980s we can catch echoes of the exuberant entrepreneurial warfare of the post–Civil War period.

The tactics were cruder in the old days, of course. In the annals of nineteenth-century corporate combat, the classic conflict was the one waged over control of the Erie railroad in 1867–68. It is a chronicle worth recalling, for few business clashes employed so extensive a repertoire of deceit and skulduggery.[1] At the outset, the antagonists appeared to be unmatched—the legendary Cornelius Vanderbilt, who had made his fortune in shipping before turning his enormous resources to railways, and two little-known young brokers, Jay Gould and Jim Fisk, whose defense of the Erie soon made them as famous as their sponsor, Daniel Drew, the predatory Wall Street short seller.

Vanderbilt controlled the New York Central line and was trying to build a system of affiliated railroads that would link New York City and

Chicago, a route obviously destined to become one of the most lucra-tive in the country. Vanderbilt's plans were threatened by the Erie, which ran from Jersey City to Buffalo, for it was also pursuing a rival net-work of routes to Chicago. To fend off the competition, Vanderbilt decided to win control of the Erie by purchasing its shares in the open market. "Buy Erie," he told his minions. "Buy it at the lowest figure you can, but buy it!"[2] He had every reason to assume he would succeed. He had plenty of money, there were only a finite number of Erie shares out-standing, and the Erie, like other railroads, was prohibited by a federal law from issuing any more stock. Vanderbilt was also aware, however, that it was legal for a railroad to issue convertible bonds and thereafter convert them to equity shares. Concerned about that danger, he had armed himself early in the struggle with an injunction from a cooperative judge in New York City, prohibiting Erie's officers and board of direc-tors from issuing convertible bonds as well as stock.

But Vanderbilt had not reckoned with the ingenuity of Gould, Fisk and Drew. The injunction did not mention the Erie executive committee, on which the three men sat, and the committee promptly issued a tor-rent of new convertible bonds—$2 million at one point, $5 million on each of two other occasions—and later converted them to stock, to be dribbled out to brokers around town. As fast as Vanderbilt's agents bought the shares, the supply increased. "If this printing press don't break down, I'll be damned if I don't give the old hog all he wants of Erie!" Jim Fisk is supposed to have boasted.[3]

When Vanderbilt discovered that he had been hoodwinked, he got his ever-obliging judge to broaden the injunction to include Erie's exec-utive committee, whereupon his opponents located a judge in Binghamton, in upstate New York, who stayed the Manhattan judge's order. Before Vanderbilt could move again, the Erie shares turned up in brokers' offices all over New York. Rather than admit defeat, Vanderbilt kept buying.

Vanderbilt's judge then ground out further injunctions and before long issued contempt citations, ordering the arrest and jailing of the entire Erie board of directors. Gould and Fisk and all but three directors fled by ferry across the Hudson to New Jersey, taking with them the corporate records, correspondence files and several million dollars in cash. A few weeks later, Gould made his way to Albany, his mission to get a bill through the New York legislature retrospectively legalizing Erie's convertible issues and all its acts. At every turn, Gould was prepared to supplement his persuasiveness with cash. There were many takers among the legislators, although Vanderbilt had his own agents on a different floor of the same hotel, fighting Gould with equivalent tokens of esteem. In the end, the Erie bill was approved by the legislature and Gould was elected president of Erie.

A year after his victory in what came to be known as the Erie wars, Gould embarked on a far more daring venture—to corner the country's gold supply (or, more precisely, that portion that was not in the vaults of the U.S. Treasury). A "corner"—control over the available supply of a security or a commodity—is one of the most difficult and rewarding of the manipulative ploys attempted by speculators on the exchanges. It is difficult because it takes a lot of money to keep buying as the price rises steadily, but the rewards are high when the time comes for the holder of the corner "to squeeze the shorts." Typically, as the price goes up, a bearish group of speculators sell short—that is, they sell borrowed securities in the hope of later buying them in the market at a lower price, thereby making a profit. If the price does not fall, the short seller takes a loss, as he is compelled to redeem the borrowed stock. His position becomes intolerable, however, when someone has achieved a corner, leaving an insufficient supply of shares available for purchase. Now comes the "squeeze," with the shorts having to pay whatever is demanded of them.

In the modern era, corners have been illegal ever since federal regulation of the securities markets began in 1934. They still occasionally occur, however, mostly in securities with a relatively small volume of shares available for trading. The Hunt brothers of Texas, however, invested billions a few years ago in what the financial world regarded as a foolhardy effort to corner the silver market. (The Hunts always denied the intent.) They lost out, however, when the price of silver plunged, and they ultimately went bankrupt. Gould was much luckier. In his day, corners were not uncommon, but no one before him was audacious enough to try to corner gold. Both Wall Street and the daily papers followed his moves with a mixture of shock and awe.

Gould's maneuvers were by no means limited to the gold room of the New York Stock Exchange. He was aware that any attempt to corner the $15 million to $20 million in gold traded in New York could be undone by the actions of the federal Treasury if it decided to step up its own sales of gold. In the spring of 1869, Gould prudently decided that "nothing could be done in gold without inside information," as Maury Klein puts it in his absorbing volume, *The Life and Legend of*

Jay Gould.[4] A series of incredible events followed. According to Klein, who bases his chronicle on a number of earlier accounts, Gould succeeded in getting a pipeline into the White House, no less, in the person of Abel R. Corbin, a New York resident who was President Ulysses S. Grant's brother-in-law.

To seal Corbin's commitment to the cause, Gould later made him a loan and still later gave his wife a cost-free investment of $1.5 million in gold. Corbin thought it inappropriate to put the investment in his own name. Corbin, for his part, won Gould an audience with the president—on a yacht in New York Harbor—but Gould was never able to persuade Grant of the economic wisdom of allowing the price of gold to soar, though for a time Gould misread the signals and thought that he had a clear field to push up the price.

To finance his purchases, he bought control of a bank in New York, which gave him a virtually open-ended supply of credit. He had a few trusted confederates and used scores of brokers to disguise his purchases. In September, he plunged heavily on the gold exchange and forced the price from $60 to a high of $165 on the final climactic day, which became known as Black Friday. "The riotous scenes that developed in exchanges all over the country were like to engulf the whole nation in ruins," Matthew Josephson wrote in *The Robber Barons*. "During the mad gyrations of the day, from Boston to San Francisco banks and brokerage houses closed their doors, while the streets of the financial centers were thronged by a milling mob. In Philadelphia, the clocklike indicator of the gold market could no longer keep up with the lightning fluctuations. . . ." Gould might have lost everything had he not gotten an inadvertent hint of prospective U.S. Treasury intervention—through Corbin, whose wife had received a letter from the president's wife. Gould managed to sell out his holdings on the last day of the rally, before the official word came that the Treasury was dumping $4 million worth of gold on the market and the price plummeted.

So Gould emerged unscathed, with a profit that was estimated to be as high as $11 million; no outsider ever knew for sure. Many other speculators, caught in the frenzy of steeply rising prices, suffered severe losses. To pull off the caper, Gould had employed inside information, bribery (he even vainly tried to bribe one of the president's secretaries), blatant self-dealing with his own bank, and manipulative tactics not only on the gold exchange but in the highest executive suite in the land. He saw President Grant a total of three times. Some of these tactics, such as bribery, were as illegal in 1869 as today, and though they shocked people, no prosecutor indicted Gould. A congressional investigation was held the following year, and that was the end of the matter.

Bribery was a commonplace in this era, and it remained a commonplace of municipal and state governments for decades to come. It is hardly unknown today, of course, but is much more discreet. Then as now, bribes were pressed on government officials by businessmen eager to secure benefits for their enterprises—a franchise, a license, a construction contract, a railway right-of-way, a piece of favorable legislation. For many elected officials, the salary that office brought was the least of its boons, far outweighed by the money that could be made by selling the favors of office.

Depending on their degree of cynicism, businessmen accepted bribery either as a standard operating procedure or as an unfortunate necessity in a pinch. Most voters were indifferent; bribery did not touch them directly, and a large proportion of the urban electorate was made up of recently arrived immigrants, loyal to the corrupt big-city political machines, to whose local leaders they looked for small favors when they got in trouble with the law or needed help in getting a job. To be sure, there were occasional eruptions of reformist zeal in the cities. Boss William Tweed, who dominated New York City politics in the 1870s, ended up in jail, his political organization shattered.[5]

It took a really big corruption scandal such as the notorious Credit Mobilier affair, which broke in 1872, to roil the country. Credit Mobilier was a construction company, set up by insiders of the Union Pacific, to finish the rail line being built westward from the Missouri River to Promontory Point, Utah. There, in May 1869, it met the Central Pacific, which had pushed out from California, giving the country its first transcontinental railway.

The use of a construction company controlled by corporate insiders was typical of the railroad barons' self-dealing; the practice vastly inflated the cost of construction and led to huge profits by the controlling group. Credit Mobilier became a public scandal because of a quarrel among its leaders, which led to the publication of an incriminating letter written by Oakes Ames, the head of the company and a Massachusetts congressman. The letter detailed the long list of Washington notables, including congressmen on both sides of the aisle, to whom Ames had given company shares or sold them at par, far below their real value. His purpose, Ames confided, was to distribute the shares "where it will produce the most good for us." At the time, he was trying to prevent a congressional investigation, but after the letter appeared there was a tremendous uproar and extensive congressional hearings. Ames was hugely embarrassed but got off with censure.[6]

Throughout this period, there was an inexorable movement toward industrial concentration through mergers, pools, trusts and holding companies, all in pursuit of increasing efficiency and the elimination of "ruinous" competition. The big businessmen of the period not only were untroubled by any common-law prohibition of restraint of trade but were less moved to utter the sort of pieties about the virtues of competition that industrialists in our more sophisticated era feel compelled to voice, however much practice contradicts precept.

In the 1870s, pools were a popular instrument to restrict competition and guarantee profits, but they had an inherent instability. Competitors would agree in a signed document to fix prices, limit output, allocate territories. The willingness of participants to sign such documents indicates that they were hardly troubled by any risk of illegality, but they were discreet enough not to publicize the agreements. Not all participants signed up voluntarily; some succumbed to the pressure of predatory pricing by more powerful competitors. Policing the arrangements presented problems, however, for there was frequently a temptation for one or another participant to cut prices to get a big order and make a quick killing. If caught, violators were fined by the pool, but if cheating became too common the pool would fall apart, often to be later reconstituted. Pools were most numerous on the railroads, but also existed in the salt industry, whisky distilling, steel, wire nails, sugar and meat packing.[7]

Trusts, which followed pools in many industries, constituted a much stronger form of organization. Eventually the term came to mean any large-scale combination that dominated an industry. Technically, however, the term referred to a specific form of organization, in which a group of trustees held the equity shares of a number of corporations in the same industry and ran the operation as one giant enterprise—cutting overhead, eliminating redundant capacity, underpricing would-be entrants to the industry, controlling output in accord with fluctuating demand—doing everything, in short, to lift prices above the level to which competition would have pushed them.

The Standard Oil Company was the first great trust. Originally a small oil refinery in Cleveland, owned by John D. Rockefeller and two associates, it expanded by buying out its two dozen competitors in Cleveland—either for cash or Standard Oil shares. Its acquisitive blitz in 1871–72 succeeded because of both Rockefeller's persuasiveness and his shrewd use of pressure tactics. Standard Oil had gotten the New York Central and other railroads to grant it substantial rebates from the stipulated freight charges that most shippers paid. Rockefeller could thus underprice his Cleveland competitors—a threat he held over anyone who would not sell out to him.

With Cleveland sewn up, Standard Oil started buying up refineries in Philadelphia, Pittsburgh and New York. Later it used its clout with the railroads to win a dominant position in the barreling and shipping of oil. It was soon in control of the earliest pipelines. It developed a superb sales organization to sell its oil directly to retail merchants. To eliminate rival wholesalers in a locality, it indulged in predatory pricing: it cut prices below cost—and then raised them after competition collapsed. In 1882, it reorganized its far-flung subsidiaries into several statewide Standard Oil companies, with the shares of all of them placed in the hands of nine trustees in New York, headed by Rockefeller. Soon afterward, the company went into oil drilling. Less than two decades after it had started expanding, the company had almost a total monopoly in its industry. The few independents counted for little.[8]

After Standard Oil showed the way, trusts were organized in lead, whisky, sugar, tobacco, rubber, copper, farm machinery, not to speak of linseed oil and cottonseed oil. The galloping trustification of America was by no means quietly accepted by the country—there were political denunciations galore, intermittent exposes in the press, state and congressional investigations. The nation's first regulatory agency, the Interstate Commerce Commission, was set up by Congress in 1887, but for years it lacked the power to eliminate economic mayhem on the railroads. Additional legislation, after the turn of the century, was required before it was able to get a grip on the problem of discriminatory rebates.

In 1890 came the first antimonopoly legislation, the Sherman Anti-Trust Act, which illegalized every "contract, combination or conspiracy in restraint of trade among the several states." The law provided no definition, however, of the actions that constituted restraint of trade and provided no enforcement machinery. The federal courts were to decide, on a case-by-case basis, with the Justice Department (and private complainants) taking the initiative in bringing cases. For several years, the act was ineffective. In 1895, in the E. C. Knight case, the Supreme Court struck a severe blow at the potency of the act by declaring that a combination of sugar producers that controlled 98 percent of the nation's refining capacity had not violated the act because it was engaged in intrastate manufacturing and not in interstate trade or commerce—the activities covered by the statute—even though the sugar was sold throughout the country.

In the long run that court decision was superseded, but for a time it encouraged the very monopolistic practices that the act was commonly thought to have prohibited. In 1899, the blind spot began to lift from the eye of justice; in the Addyston Pipe and Steel Company case, the Court of Appeals for the Sixth Circuit outlawed a bid-rigging conspiracy among a group of pipe manufacturers, and the Supreme Court affirmed it, after modification. Soon after Theodore Roosevelt acceded to the presidency, he launched an assault against the trusts. In 1902, he directed the attorney general to proceed against the Northern Securities Company, a holding company recently established to control two mighty railroads, the Union Pacific and the Northern Pacific. In 1904, when the Supreme Court ordered the dissolution of Northern Securities, the trustbusters could hail a major victory.[9]

Even more significant divestitures came in 1911, with the Supreme Court ordering both the Standard Oil Company and the American Tobacco Company to be broken up into their constituent elements. In the end, the puny instrument of the Sherman Anti-Trust Act proved to be a potent weapon. Then in 1914, Congress passed the Clayton Act, which proscribed a variety of anticompetitive practices, some of which prohibitions lawyers and economists later came to regard as counterproductive.

Antitrust legislation and adverse court decisions did not change the propensity of businessmen to fix prices and thus boost profits. Such inclinations remained, as a long line of recent cases clearly proves, but in later years they have had to be indulged in a more discreet, not to say covert, fashion. No one can doubt that any lapse in law enforcement would encourage an exuberant degree of recidivism.

Saul Engelbourg, in *Power and Morality: American Business Ethics, 1840–1914*, has persuasively argued that by the second decade of the twentieth century, businessmen had gradually developed some rudimentary concern for ethical propriety, in such matters as less cavalier treatment of shareholders, less secrecy about corporate affairs, and less tolerance for blatant self-dealing.[10] Certainly, nobody any longer practiced the flamboyant kind of corporate warfare of a Commodore Vanderbilt or a Jay Gould. In a battle for control of a corporation, one might try to dilute an opponent's ownership stake in the target company's shares, but not by the simple tactic of running off more stock on the company's printing press. And bribery of public officials was handled with much more discretion than in the Erie wars.

Wall Street, however, remained a jungle, or an unregulated gambling casino—both shopworn but accurate metaphors. During the boom years of the 1920s, the financial markets were not only infected with a speculative mania but regularly operated with a degree of mendacity, manipulation and malpractice far in excess of the levels of delinquency in the 1970s and 1980s. Before the SEC was created in 1934, trading on inside information was rife, conflict of interest was a commonplace, and devious techniques were regularly employed to run stock prices up and down.

In floating new issues, investment banks frequently exploited the unwary buyer. In contrast to the requirement of full disclosure that came in with the New Deal reforms, underwriters practiced what might cynically be called plausible disclosure—just enough facts or presumed facts to beguile the investor into putting down some money. The selling of foreign bond issues was a particular scandal, as the Senate Banking Committee noted in its 1934 report on an exhaustive, two-year investigation of the securities markets—an inquiry generally known as the Pecora investigation, after its chief counsel, Ferdinand Pecora.

Between March 1, 1927, and October 1928, for example, the securities affiliate of the National City Bank of New York, together with several other eminent investment houses, sold three issues of Peruvian government bonds—for $15 million, $50 million, and $25 million—considerable sums in those days. The market gobbled them up. It was good business for the investment banks, since they shared a commission of 5 percent or more. But by 1931, all three issues were in default and selling at a tiny fraction of their original value.

More than worldwide depression accounted for the debacle. Peru had been an appalling credit risk when the bonds were issued, a fact recognized in innumerable communiques that National City Bank received from its representatives in Peru between 1921 and 1928. The country was laggard in paying its debts; its economy was shaky; its natural resources were largely foreign owned, leaving little wealth in the country—and it was politically unstable to boot.[11] Not a word about any of these dismal circumstances appeared in any of the underwriters' prospectuses. The Senate committee report outlined similar selective disclosure in several other Cuban, Chilean, and Brazilian debt issues, all of which went belly-up.[12]

During the 1920s, the pool became one of the most popular manipulative devices available to the Wall Street professional. In nineteenth-century parlance, as noted, a pool was an agreement among competitors to fix prices. On the stock markets, however, a pool became the generic term for an agreement between several parties to trade a particular security in such a way as to create deceptive price movements and thereby generate trading profits, which the pool members shared. Typically, the pool would select a company that in some fashion was in the news, either for expected rising earnings, an anticipated dividend increase, or a hot new product. A pool would normally be run by a professional manager; its participants, who contributed to a joint trading account, would often include one or more insiders from the target corporation. While some pools were set up to defend a stock that was threatened by a "bear raid"—that is, a concerted effort to drive down its price by selling it short—most pools sought to boost a stock's price through synthetic trading activity.

Not to tip his hand, the pool manager would initiate a widely dispersed series of trades in the targeted stock, using several brokers in different cities to buy and sell shares. More shares would be bought than sold, for the pool manager wanted to accumulate a block of stock while the price was still low; thereafter, the point of parallel sales was to keep the price from shooting up too fast, and also to simulate the appearance of normal trading as the transactions were recorded on the tape in brokers' offices.

The carefully orchestrated trades, in mounting volume and gradually ascending prices, would go on for days or weeks in the hope that outside traders watching the tape would be encouraged by the action to start buying shares on their own, leading to a sharp run-up in price. At the same time, public interest in the stock would be fueled by the floating of rumors and planting of newspaper stories concerning future developments;

on occasion, newspaper reporters were bribed to publish favorable items. That corporate insider who participated in the pool was exceedingly useful as a source of reliable tips.

Once the public was sufficiently enticed, the pool manager had little to do but monitor the situation and make a few judicious purchases when the price began to flatten. At some point, the manager had to decide whether the price had risen as high as it plausibly could, at which point it was time to take profits. This delicate operation was often called "pulling the plug," but it was best not done abruptly. If the pool suddenly dumped massive quantities of shares on the market, the price was likely to drop precipitously. Better to sell in smaller quantities, with the price descending gradually.[13]

Remarkably, all this manipulative activity was legal, in accordance with the rules of the New York Stock Exchange, the nation's largest securities market. The exchange did regard "wash sales"—offsetting buying and selling of a security by the same individual—as improper, as were "matched orders," in which separate parties did the same thing. But a coordinated plan involving several people to produce similar synthetic activity, while avoiding the precision of wash sales, was held to be unobjectionable.

So testified Richard Whitney, president of the New York Stock Exchange, when he was called before the Senate Banking Committee. At one point, committee counsel Pecora asked Whitney whether it was possible "for a group to operate in the market as to more or less control prices for the time being." Whitney replied that it was possible—"if the stock and their money hold out." Moreover, he said that "if there are no improper transactions [by which he meant wash sales] the exchange does not object." Pecora pressed on, "These persons are enabled to exercise control, are they not?" Whitney: "By bidding and offering, yes." Pecora: "Now, what steps, if any, does the exchange take to prevent that kind of control?" Whitney: "I do not know of any, Mr. Pecora."[14]

There were some on Wall Street, however, who differentiated between "nefarious" and "beneficent" pools. A nefarious operation was one whose sole purpose was to run up the price of a security at the expense of deluded outside investors. A beneficent pool, on the other hand, had as its purpose the stabilization of the market price so that a large block of stock—say, from the settlement of an estate—could be unloaded on the exchange without depressing its price. But as the

Senate committee report pointed out, "From the viewpoint of the purchaser outside the pool circle, there is no substantial or ethical difference in these two types of pool. Although the purpose may be different, the means employed are identical. In all cases, fictitious activity
is intentionally created, and the purchaser is deceived by the appearance of genuine demand for the security. Motive furnishes no justifi-
cation for the employment of manipulative devices."[15]

To their participants, pools were so beneficial that the mechanism
became widely popular. In 1929, which witnessed the peaking of the great
bull market, pools, syndicates and joint accounts—they amounted to much
the same—were created in 105 securities on the New York Stock
Exchange, according to the Senate committee report. Some of the
biggest and most prestigious U.S. corporations witnessed the manipu-
lation of their securities—among them the Allegany Corporation,
American Sugar Refining, American Tobacco, Bendix Aviation,
Bethlehem Steel, Borden, Chrysler, Consolidated Cigar, Continental Can,
Crosley Radio, Goodrich, R. H. Macy, Monsanto Chemical, National
Cash Register, Standard Oil of California, Union Carbon & Carbide,
U.S. Rubber. After the crash in October, pool activity declined, but the
committee still found such operations in 31 stocks on the NYSE in 1930.
During 1932, only two issues were the target of pools. Among member
firms on the NYSE, there was widespread participation in pool activi-
ties, with 175 firms sharing profits and losses during the period from January
1, 1929, to August 31, 1933.[16]

Some of the pools became legendary after investigators pored over
their records and brought participants before the committee. The sen-
ators discovered, for example, that a 1929 pool in the shares of Chase
National Bank, run by the brokerage house of Dominick and Dominick,
netted its participants $1,452,314.68 in a period of less than four months
of active trading. What was especially noteworthy was the participation
in the pool of both the bank and Albert H. Wiggin, its chairman.[17]

In all, the committee found that the Chase Securities Corporation,
the bank's investment banking arm, participated in eight pools in its own
stock in the four-year period September 1927 to July 1931. By using a
family corporation as his vehicle, Wiggin kept his involvement discreetly
hidden until the Senate committee laid bare the record. As Pecora later
related in his book, *Wall Street Under Oath*, in his testimony before the
committee, "Mr. Wiggin could not be brought to admit that there was

the slightest impropriety in the bank's encouragement of and participation in the gigantic pools in its own stock." The primary interest of the bank, according to Wiggin, was in "stabilizing the market," attracting more share-holders, "providing purchasing power," and having a "steadying effect" on the shares of the Chase National Bank.[18]

During the same period, Wiggin also traded privately—outside the pools—taking advantage of the skewed markets produced by the pools, and made a profit of $10,425,000. The biggest chunk of that came between September 19 and December 11, 1929, when he enriched himself to the extent of $4 million by selling his own bank's stock short. Chase's shares plummeted in the October market crash; Wiggin was either prescient or just lucky when he went short in September. But the extraordinary fact was that he did not blanch at the blatant conflict of interest and betrayal of fiduciary responsibility involved in giving him-self a financial stake in the decline of his own bank's fortunes. When the facts came to light, Wiggin felt compelled to relinquish the $100,000-a-year pension that the board of directors had voted him upon retire-ment. There was nothing illegal, however, either in trading his own stock or in using inside information about forthcoming corporate developments to time his trades most advantageously.[19]

One of the most successful pool operations of the period involved the stock of the Sinclair Consolidated Oil Corporation, headed by Harry F. Sinclair. In 1928, Sinclair wanted to raise around $30 million in new equity for his company. Nothing unusual about that, but the normal way to make such a stock offering would have been to engage an investment bank to underwrite the issue and sell it to the public through brokerage houses around the country. The investment bank would have charged a commission, of course—perhaps 3 or 4 percent. To avoid the charge, and to make a private killing on the deal himself, Sinclair approached Arthur W. Cutten to manage a pool to sell the Sinclair shares on the stock exchange. The plan was simple: the pool would buy the shares from the company and then peddle them on the exchange at a profit. The original pool members consisted of Cutten and Sinclair, each with a one-quarter interest, with the remainder divided between Blair & Co., a bro-kerage house, Chase Securities Corporation, and the Shermar Corporation (Cutten and Sinclair later parceled out subparticipations to various friends and associates.) This group constituted the purchasing syndicate, so called because it bought 1,130,000 shares from the oil company at $30 each. At the same time, the group formed a second pool—a trading syndicate—to "maintain" the price of Sinclair Oil if it seemed subject to serious erosion.

In this case, no secret was made of Arthur Cutten's participation as pool manager. Indeed, his active management of the deal was initially heralded, for he was regarded as a deft market operator with a long string of successes. Public interest in Sinclair Oil was immediately evident. The Senate Banking Committee report points out that on October 24, 1928—on the very day that the syndicate agreements were signed and before the pools could actively trade—the price of Sinclair stock opened at 32 and moved to 34 3/4 at the close of the day. Cutten's name was such a magnet that the public was clearly not deterred by any fear of a distorted market. The irony throughout this period was that while the outside investor was frequently fleeced by manipulative practices, he was often an eager participant in his own victimization. Like visitors to a gambling casino who know that the odds are stacked against them, many investors hoped to be nimble enough or lucky enough to ride up a stock while it had pool support and get out in time. Some were successful. Others were caught in the downdraft.

Both the purchasing and the trading syndicates actively bought and sold Sinclair shares, aggressively pushing its price upward, with the public following in train. Much of the activity was in the range of $38 to $45 per share. On a typical day, November 5, 1928, 210,000 shares were traded, with the purchasing syndicate selling 100,600 shares and buying 11,600, while the trading syndicate bought 50,900. "On many other days," according to the Senate committee report, "the activities of the accounts bordered perilously upon the forbidden domain of 'wash' sales."

The purchasing syndicate wound up its affairs in April 1929, six months after it started. It had not only sold out its initial allotment of 1,130,000 shares but another 700,000 as well, bought on the exchange. Its profit, according to the Senate committee, was $12,200,109.41. The following month, the trading syndicate ended its activities, having purchased and sold 634,000 shares, with a profit of $418,383.54. All told, a profit of nearly $13 million for six months' work, most of it by the pool manager. Multiply by nine or ten to translate into today's dollars.[20]

Not the least of the delinquencies of the pool operators was the occasional corruption of the press. A fringe of financial journalists were not averse to touting stocks that were the subject of pool manipulations, in return for honoraria in one form or another. The Senate committee received several intriguing pieces of testimony on the subject and concluded that "it was usual and customary for the operators to pay newspaper writers for publicity and propaganda disguised as financial news. The compensation was paid in the form of cash or options on the securities so publicized."

Among the sinners who testified before the committee was one David M. Lion, publisher of an enterprising journal called *The Stock and Bond Reporter*, which specialized in boosting the securities of pool operators, who compensated him with call options. As an additional service to his clients, Lion employed William J. McMahon, one of the earliest purveyors of financial advice over the airwaves. McMahon, billed as an economist and president of the McMahon Institute of Financial Research, would talk authoritatively about trends in the market, in the course of which he would throw in a plug or two for whatever stock Lion was currently promoting. Lion paid McMahon $250 a week—well above $2,000 a week in today's dollars. Lion testified that he also employed a stable of newspapermen to push his stocks on an ad hoc basis. He had a lot of work to dole out: during the course of 1928–30 he was retained by some 250 pools. In all, he made a profit of $500,000 for three years of labor.[21]

Nothing in the modern era can quite equal the ethical debauchery, betrayal of fiduciary responsibility, and general bamboozlement of the public that characterized Wall Street in the 1920s (although the insider trading scandals of the 1980s come closest). But as remarkable as the widespread flimflammery was the candor with which it was practiced and defended. The basic reason has already been alluded to: most of the delinquency was not illegal. To be sure, there were state "blue-sky" laws to protect the public from the sale of fraudulent securities (the laws were so called because of the penchant of unscrupulous promoters to promise the heavens). But enforcement was ineffective: if one state cracked down, the promoters simply moved to another.

More significant was the lack of regulation of the securities exchanges, except by themselves, which led to a tolerance of manipulative practices and a breathtaking suspension of moral scruples. Even when there were laws, such as those regarding bribery or the fiduciary responsibility of boards of directors, there was no national authority to police the field and bring culprits to book.

All that changed, of course, with the enactment of the Securities Act of 1933 and the Securities Exchange Act of 1934. The first required the registration of securities issues, together with the disclosure to potential buyers of all relevant information about the issuing corporation, including past balance sheets and profit and loss statements. The Securities Exchange Act imposed federal registration of all securities exchanges and of the broker-dealers who traded on them. (Over-the-counter dealers were later added.) The commission set up by the act had the ultimate authority over all the regulations of the exchanges; in 1938, the Securities and Exchange Commission forced a complete reorganization of the New York Stock Exchange. The 1934 act also outlawed such manipulative techniques as pools and wash sales and imposed rules on the trading by corporate insiders in the shares of their own companies; it also forbade them to sell their own companies' stock short. The commission was authorized to keep the markets under continual surveillance and was armed with a variety of disciplinary sanctions.[22]

The new regime of federal regulation soon transformed the practices of the exchanges. The blatant abuses—bear raids, pools, corners, misleading stock prospectuses—disappeared, at least as highly visible phenomena. Over the years, the SEC has generated a vast body of regulation and precedent. Violators are frequently fined, suspended or tossed out of the securities industry. Sometimes they go to jail. In light of all the prohibitions, it is reasonable to regard the great wave of violations recently uncovered—such as massive insider trading and stock "parking" for various illegal purposes—as more egregious than the old capers, though far less flamboyant.

Of what relevance to present conditions, however, are the horror stories of the past? Paradoxically, they can be taken as reassuring, to a degree (inasmuch as they have disappeared). They also provide a guide to future action. For the excesses of Wall Street, like the depredations of the nineteenth-century monopolists, led over a period of time to widespread public clamor for intervention by the national government, the only authority with sufficient power to impose adequate restraints. First the Sherman Act and then the Clayton Act provided the legal means to ensure competition in the marketplace and were on occasion impressive in their effectiveness. Later came the securities laws of the 1930s, which revolutionized the way Wall Street does business. None of these laws were cure-alls, as has become obvious in recent years, with new problems and scandals requiring additional remedies. But the record of the past suggests that legal prohibitions, backed up by zealous enforcement, can significantly alter corporate behavior. That is indeed reassuring.

CHAPTER 3

THE JOLLY BAND OF

PRICE FIXERS

Antitrust is a highly contentious field, with endless arguments over the degree of concentration in an industry that should trigger government action, the propriety of vertical integration, even whether predatory pricing is illegal under all circumstances. The political right is far less interventionist than the left in antitrust philosophy, as in other matters, and does not equate bigness with badness, to put it crudely. Thus, during the Reagan years, the Justice Department's antitrust division challenged few of the spectacular corporate mergers that restructured American capitalism. The division saw no threat—and perhaps heightened economic efficiencies—in these consolidations, whereas traditional trustbusters would probably have feared an inexorable tendency toward monopoly.

But on one issue there is no disagreement between right and left, between the Chicago school of economic and legal scholars and the liberal trustbusters: collusive price-fixing and bid rigging are regarded by everyone as foul play, bereft of any redeeming virtue, on the grounds that they subvert the free market and impose an unjustifiable burden on consumers. No antitrust theorist utters a word in exculpation of price-fixing, and few suggest that the criminal penalties to which it is subject are inappropriate.[1] By contrast, other antitrust infractions bring civil penalties—prohibitions, divestitures, consent decrees. Ever since a string of major price-fixing convictions in the electrical manufacturing industry in 1960, judges have shown an increasing tendency to send culprits to prison. In 1974, Congress raised criminal violations from a misdemeanor to a felony, fixing maximum penalties at $1 million in fines for corporations and three years in prison for individuals. An act of Congress in the fall of 1990 increased the maximum corporate fine to $10 million.[2]

Despite the risks, price-fixing remains an activity of contagious appeal and stubborn persistence, which makes it a central concern of this book (unlike civil antitrust issues, which are beyond our scope). The attraction of price-fixing is easy to understand: it is a simple way of minimizing one of the major hazards of doing business—price competition. While competitive markets are cherished by academic economists, businessmen often weary of the swift race. Competition breeds uncertainty; it can lead to low or nil profits and can even result in the demise of some of the players. Collusive price-fixing, by contrast, offers the benign appeal of cooperation (a euphemism at times employed by members of price-fixing rings), even the warm glow of fraternity. By long convention, someone who refuses to join the brotherhood, or defects and undercuts the price, is scorned as a chiseler. Viewed from the outside, of course, the chiseler is just someone who obeys the law.

The public interest in curbing price-fixing is obvious: the practice victimizes consumers by boosting prices above the level that competition would set. Price fixers often claim that they don't "gouge" customers—that is, they do not exact every last dollar obtainable without reducing demand for their products. But clearly they inflate prices above the market level, for that is the whole point of the exercise. And to the extent that prices are raised artificially, the public loses—it is a zero-sum game—whether the consumer is a corporate entity or an individual. Price-fixing also promotes inefficiency, for a cartel price tends to be pegged at a level where it will protect inefficient as well as efficient producers. A cartel indulges the less competent because it must include almost all competitors in order to be effective.

The precise economic toll of any particular price-fixing conspiracy is not easy to discover. In a criminal case, it is necessary to prove only that illegal price-fixing occurred; the amount of overcharge is incidental. In a civil suit for triple damages following a criminal conviction, however, the extent of the plaintiff's loss is the crucial matter. Most of these suits are settled out of court, but the size of the settle-

ment—obviously less than the full entitlement—gives some indica-
tion of the economic cost of the price-fixing effort. The first chapter
of the book mentioned one of the largest settlements on record—$550
million received by some nine thousand purchasers of corrugated
boxes from a group of manufacturers who had conspired to rig prices
over several years.

There were other large settlements as well in a series of cases in the
forest products industries that first began in the 1970s. Plaintiffs who sued
a group of price-fixing plywood manufacturers collected more than
$175 million. A class action suit against folding carton producers
brought $200 million. Even manufacturers of what the industry calls "fine
paper" had to fork up $50 million. Other large settlements were paid by
manufacturers of antibiotics ($196 million), gypsum wallboard ($75 million), and chlorine ($50 million).[3]

By the nature of things, no one can know the full extent of price-
fixing and bid rigging in the economy, but when a big case—or a cluster of cases—breaks, its ramifications can be startling: a whole industry affecting vast reaches of the economy is often involved. That was
true of the price-fixing conspiracies in the heavy electrical equipment
industry alluded to earlier that culminated in the 1960 convictions of
General Electric, Westinghouse, Allis-Chalmers, and a number of less
well known companies, together with many of their executives, who
had routinely fixed prices for years on a variety of products. It was the
biggest antitrust scandal up to that time because of both its range and
the renown of its leading participants.[4] There was also industrywide involvement in a price-fixing cabal in the plumbing fixtures industry in the 1960s,[5]
in many later conspiracies in the forest products industries, and most
recently in a continuing series of cases in electrical construction (as dis-
tinguished from equipment manufacturing). That scandal involved
bid rigging on the electrical work for major construction projects—electrical generating plants, some of them nuclear, as well as steelworks and
water treatment plants.

As briefly mentioned in the first chapter, the investigation into electrical construction practices was triggered by the arrival of a letter addressed
to William Baxter, then chief of the antitrust division of the Justice
Department. It was an astonishing document, not at all the kind of
vaguely worded, emotionally overwrought complaint, perhaps tinged
with a hint of paranoia, that regularly descends on enforcement

agencies. Instead, in brisk, businesslike language, the letter charged that the nation's leading electrical contractors had routinely violated the antitrust laws by phonying bids on large construction jobs. It named companies and provided details of bid rigging on a dozen projects. Clearly, this was not the effusion of some nut but of a whistle-blower intimately acquainted with the industry, whatever his private grievances.[6]

Baxter soon afterward launched a broad investigation; the payoff was not long in coming and it was huge. From May 1983 through June 1992, the antitrust division initiated 102 criminal prosecutions, involving 100 corporations in the District of Columbia and 14 states spanning the nation, from New Jersey and Pennsylvania to California and Washington. In the overwhelming majority of the cases—a total of 77—the government's evidence was so strong that the accused pled guilty. In some of those cases, as well as in some others, 21 companies and 8 individuals were allowed by the courts to plead nolo contendere—which results in automatic conviction, as does a guilty plea, but has a more ambiguous ring to it, allowing the accused company to claim, however implausibly, that it was really innocent but preferred not to stand the expense or hazard of trial.* Only 16 cases had to go to trial; 10 corporations and 17 individuals were convicted, and 6 corporations and 10 individuals were acquitted. The penalties: fines totaling $28.4 million and prison sentences involving actual incarceration of more than 13 years. There were several million-dollar fines and one of $1,501,000 levied against individual companies. The antitrust division is still actively pursuing the price-fixing cabals, with three grand juries still impaneled.[7]

Most of the nation's large electrical construction companies in business in the 1980s have been convicted, some more than once—among them Fischbach and Moore, Lord Electric, E. C. Ernst, Sargent Electric, the Howard P. Foley Company, Commonwealth Electric, as well as many smaller companies.[8] The violations did not constitute one giant nationwide conspiracy, but a series of local conspiracies in which many of the national companies participated through their branch offices.

---

* Moreover, a nolo plea is helpful to the defendant should there be a later suit for civil damages, for nolo is not taken as proof of culpability, as is a prior guilty plea. The plaintiff in the civil suit thus has the burden of proving that the offense occurred as well as proving the extent of damages.

The electrical contracting cases, classic examples of bid rigging at its most artful, illustrate how even the most discreet schemes can be unraveled by the methodical investigative techniques of the antitrust division. The first step, after the incriminating letter arrived on Baxter's desk, was to convene a grand jury in Washington, D.C., where one of the suspect companies had its headquarters.

More grand juries were later convened in other cities. Guided by the letter's specific accusations, the government lawyers followed their normal practice of subpoenaing all corporate records relating to the suspected rigged bids—the actual bidding documents, the cost estimate sheets prepared by the company's estimators (to see if someone later altered them to justify a higher bid), and various bits and pieces of paper—such as expense records, daily diaries, telephone bills, telephone message slips—that could document how key players communicated with each other at crucial points in the conspiracy.

Initially, the government summoned mid-level executives from the target companies—mainly individuals who had handled the background documents for the bidding but did not participate in the rigging, though they might have information about it. As the antitrust lawyers' knowledge of a case grew, their questions became more detailed, and they often received candid answers from people who were loath to perjure themselves but might have stonewalled more general questions.

The next step was to immunize lower-level participants in the plot in return for testimony against their superiors. At this stage, rumors usually circulate about the case the government is building, and there is often a competitive rush to the courthouse to obtain immunity. It is sometimes also offered to one or more of the ringleaders, if that is the best way to get needed testimony against confederates. As the results show, the government's investigators performed with skill and thoroughness.

The bid-rigging schemes followed a pattern. Most of the major players in the industry met periodically to determine who would receive the large jobs. Typically, the plot got under way after the customer distributed a "bidders list" naming the companies invited to compete. The selection was generally based on an assessment of their qualifications; few companies, for example, had the skill to work on a nuclear power plant. "Once you had the bidders list, then you made the decision as to how the job would be allocated," says Hays Gorey, Jr., an antitrust division lawyer who helped crack the cases. "The other questions were—where is the job, who was interested

in it, who was due a favor based on past favors? Quite often they didn't readily agree. Often the meetings would be somewhat contentious."

The contractor who wanted the job would seek "support" from the
others. "If you got the support of everyone," Gorey remarks, "that meant
that you had eliminated all the competition." In the final day or two before
the bids were due, there would be further conversations about setting
the dollar range for the bids that were designed to be too high; it was
vital that the distribution look normal to the customer. Sometimes the
anointed lower bidder wouldn't announce his actual price, for fear that
someone might betray him by underbidding, but would tell his co-
conspirators the approximate prices they should quote. Occasionally
there was contention about who should be the second-lowest bidder, for
if the lowest bidder was later disqualified for some reason, the runner-
up would automatically get the work.[9]

In 1984, Gorey was the lead government lawyer on a major bid-
rigging case in Pittsburgh that involved not a single big construction
job but a series of projects over many years for U.S. Steel's Western
Pennsylvania works. The government believed that the conspiracy dated
back to the 1960s ("handed down from generation to generation," according to Gorey), but the indictment only listed the period from 1974
to 1981, during which it charged that fifty-nine contracts with a
total value of $23.5 million had been rigged by the defendants.

To get the best price, U.S. Steel always solicited bids from five or six
companies. The contractors, however, subverted the process by acting
in concert on all but the smallest jobs. The rigged jobs were generally
in the range of $500,000 to $1.5 million; the most expensive project cost
$5 million. One of the companies in the ring maintained a suite at the
Duquesne Club, an old-line businessmen's club in downtown Pittsburgh
within walking distance of most of the contractors, which became the
venue for their plotting. The group met ten to fifteen times a year, as
frequently as U.S. Steel had contracts to let.

The plotters were discreet. When one of them wanted a meeting, he
would telephone and say something like "Let's meet for coffee at the usual
place." If the person being called was not at his desk, the caller would
leave only his first name. The members of the group would arrive and
leave separately, and they devised a cover story if an outsider inadver-
tently walked into the meeting: they were at a local session of their national trade association.

It was a smooth-running system, highly profitable all around. Over the years, each job's profit was 10 to 15 percent higher than it would otherwise have been, according to a witness at the trial who had been privy to the operation but later decided to cooperate with the government. One of the companies pled guilty, after bargaining for terms, another pled nolo contendere and testified for the government, three others were convicted after trial, and one was acquitted. Four of the companies were fined $1 million each; three of the executives were each sentenced to ninety days.

Ironically, until the case broke, U.S. Steel was apparently unaware that it had been cheated of millions in excess charges. The conspirators had prided themselves on charging "reasonable" prices, but there is no sense in attributing charitable motives to them: had they charged extortionate prices their customer would doubtless have become suspicious.

The only time the bidding was honest was when the jobs were too modest to be worth finagling or when certain small companies were included on the list of prospective bidders. The jolly band of Duquesne Club conspirators knew that these outsiders would not cooperate.[10]

Not all industries, of course, are prone to bid rigging and price-fixing. It is not likely to occur in an industry with many competitors or with highly differentiated products—for example, clothing manufacturing. Traditionally, entry into the industry has been easy for newcomers because of relatively low capital requirements. A multiplicity of enterprises obviously makes it difficult to impose the discipline of a price-fixing agreement—except perhaps in the case of a large government order for a specified product, for which only a small number of firms bid. But it would be a heroic task to fix prices on clothing sold to stores. Apart from the large number of available manufacturers, style differences make for a line of products that is too variegated. In sum, two basic characteristics make an industry vulnerable to price-fixing conspiracies—a high degree of corporate concentration and a relatively undifferentiated product.

Both are exemplified in full measure by the soft drink industry, in which some producers have had a harrowing encounter with the Sherman Act in recent years. Since the mid-1980s, the antitrust division has uncovered a series of price-fixing arrangements between purveyors of Coca-Cola and Pepsi-Cola, the two goliaths that dominate the market for cola beverages.

The parent companies were not involved in the illegalities; the offenders were regional bottlers, who buy syrup from the parent company and manufacture, bottle and market the drink. As in so many instances, the case began fortuitously, through an isolated complaint. A man named Ted Rivers, a motel operator in Virginia Beach, got into a dispute with a marketing representative of Mid-Atlantic Coca-Cola. The bottler was raising the price of the drink cans that Rivers bought for his automatic vending machines. Rivers protested and threatened to switch his business to Pepsi, whereupon the marketing rep told him that there was no point in changing, for the two bottlers had an agreement to quote the same price.

Rivers thought that this innocent revelation was very odd indeed and reported the matter to a friend on the Norfolk police force. The tip was later passed to the FBI and ultimately found its way to the antitrust division. But some hard evidence beyond Rivers's account was needed before a formal inquiry could be launched. Rivers was encouraged to arrange a telephone conversation with the Coca-Cola representative and agreed to tape it. The woman repeated the statement. It was hardly conclusive proof but sufficiently incriminating to launch a grand jury investigation, which was directed by a veteran antitrust lawyer, David Jordan. The long grind of interviewing witnesses and subpoenaing persons and documents was followed by immunizing three executives to get their testimony. In the end the two bottlers—Mid-Atlantic Coca-Cola and Allegheny Bottling, which sold Pepsi—stood convicted, as were several executives. Mid-Atlantic pled guilty in a pretrial agreement and paid a fine of $1 million. A seven-week trial led to the conviction of three executives, including Allegheny's controlling shareholder, Morton M. Lapides, who had put the corporation together by buying up and amalgamating several local bottling companies. The inspiration for the whole affair had clearly come from the top.*

The conspiracy covered fixing the prices of Coca-Cola and Pepsi products in parts of Maryland, Virginia, Georgia, and the District

---

* The defendants appealed the conviction, received an adverse ruling from the Fourth Circuit Court of Appeals in January 1989, and were denied a hearing by the Supreme Court in October 1989. More than two years later, in January 1992, Lapides and Alleco, Inc., as his old company was now called, filed a motion to vacate judgment on the grounds that they had been denied their Sixth Amendment rights to a fair trial. The government opposed the motion, which was still pending six months later.

of Columbia during the years 1982–85. The method was simple: Each company routinely sent its customers monthly promotional letters in which it set forth discounts from its formal prices on various drinks in return for some minimal promotional effort by the customer, such as putting up a display sign. This schedule of prices and discounts embodied the agreed price; no further discounts were to be permitted. Prior to the agreement, both bottlers had indulged in "deep discounts"—further price cuts beyond those in the monthly schedule—which escalated into price wars and horrified top executives in both companies. "The initial goal of the price fixing was to stop 'deep discounting'. . .[but it] resulted in stabilizing and fixing the price of soft drinks in the Richmond, Norfolk and Baltimore areas," observed the district court judge in denying motions for a new trial. "The government presented overwhelming evidence of a price fixing conspiracy."[11]

While corporate concentration vastly simplifies the effort to put together a price-fixing ring, a successful combine can at times be achieved without it. The rash of cases in the forest products field in the 1970s supports the point. There were dozens of significant manufacturers of corrugated boxes and folding cartons, for example, though fewer in plywood. On the other hand, the products in these industries could hardly have been more standardized; one manufacturer's box of a certain size and strength is no different from another's. The industry had an additional characteristic that prompted price-fixing and even made it seem like salvation: profit margins were thin and competition was fierce.

In bid-rigging cases, product differentiation is again absent, for all the presumed competitors are asked to bid on the same specifications set forth by the customer. In the asphalt road construction cases mentioned briefly in the first chapter, the potential competitors in each bidding contest were generally limited to three or four companies. The reason: hot asphalt is not portable for much over fifty miles from the plant where it is made because it thereafter becomes cool and cannot be laid. This technical limitation greatly narrowed the field of potential competitors, making it easier for the handful of companies pursuing each job to control the price. But there was plenty of work for each of them on a rotating basis, for highway contracts in a state are typically offered for bidding several times a year.

The widespread popularity of collusion in highway construction is indicated by the statistics. From December 1979 through June 1992, the antitrust division began 347 criminal prosecutions in 25 states. In 265 cases, the defendants pled guilty; nolo contendere pleas were accepted from 21 corporations and 14 individuals. Sixty-seven trials were held, resulting in the conviction of 34 companies and the acquittal of 38. One trial remained to be held at the close of the period surveyed. Fines totaled $66 million, with culprits sentenced to an aggregate of more than 61 years in prison.[12]

The cases had started modestly in 1979 with reports of suspicious activity in Tennessee and Virginia, as previously mentioned, and gradually snowballed. Typically, after the Justice Department got a number of indictments in one state, it would turn up informants who tipped it to similar conniving elsewhere. The convictions spread like an unquenchable inkblot across the map, reaching as far north as Vermont, as far west as the Dakotas, and as far south as Louisiana and Texas.[13] How long might these collusive practices have continued, had Justice not received the initial tips about Virginia and Tennessee?

Price-fixing flourishes not only because of its obvious benefits to participating companies but because it is perceived as relatively harmless by the individuals who negotiate the agreements. As Robert S. Bennett, a veteran white-collar defense lawyer in Washington, D.C., points out, "They see antitrust as a victimless crime. 'Who is hurt if we get together on the price of chickens? Okay, it's not the lowest price, but it's a fair price.' And, of course, in some industries you don't work if you don't fix prices."[14] The price fixers are clearly not troubled by the technical difficulty of determining a "fair" price in the absence of competition; they are practical men of affairs, not economists.

In 1978 a fascinating article appeared in the *Harvard Business Review* by Jeffrey Sonnenfeld and Paul L. Lawrence, who sought to analyze why mid- and lower-level employees in the folding carton industry had cooperated so diligently in fixing prices. For one thing, there was a tradition in the industry to collude because competition was stiff, profit margins were modest, and, while one box was like another box, specifications differed so much from one order to the next that many lower-ranking employees were involved in determining how to price a job. They could conspire with their counterparts in other companies without their bosses being aware of their activities (although the bosses, who could be presumed to know the mores of the industry, should have suspected what was going on). The authors interviewed many of the participants, one of whom uttered the classic self-justification of the price fixer: "We're not vicious enemies in this industry, but rather people in similar binds. I've always thought of myself as an honorable citizen. We didn't do these things for our own behalf . . . [but] for the betterment of the company."[15]

A year after the celebrated convictions in heavy electrical equipment in 1960, the Senate Judiciary Committee's Subcommittee on Antitrust and Monopoly, headed by Senator Estes Kefauver, held hearings to which a long string of chastened violators were summoned. Most of them were mid-level managers who had attended meetings with competitors and made the price-fixing deals. (The government was never able to pin responsibility on any of the corporate chieftains.) After the event, the managers were voluble in their expressions of regret and had a variety of explanations. They had been instructed by their superiors to go to such meetings; many had attended for years. Did they know such activity was illegal? Responded one Westinghouse sales manager: "Illegal? Yes, but not criminal. I didn't find that out until I read the indictment."[16] The sales manager of one of the smaller companies, asked whether he had been conscious of violating the antitrust laws, answered that he had been aware of the law but excused himself on the ground that "these things have been going on for some years" and that "morally it did not seem quite as bad as might be inferred by the definition of the act itself" because no customers had been defrauded or charged "excessive prices."[17]

The Westinghouse man spoke eloquently to the same theme: "I assumed that criminal action meant damaging someone, injuring someone, and we did not do that. We never quoted price that wasn't in accord with or below our published prices, which I considered to be quite fair and equitable under the circumstances, and on the basis that we were merely trying to protect ourselves from sharp purchasing practices and a competitive situation where everyone had overcapacity and there wasn't sufficient volume in the market."[18]

At least one executive at General Electric, however, lost his job as a marketing manager because of his refusal to play the game. He had signed a corporate policy statement about not meeting with competitors and, as his boss put it, he "was so religious that since he had signed this piece of paper, he decided he had to observe it." The boss commented, "He was not broad enough for the job."[19]

The antitrust division has compiled an impressive record in its criminal prosecutions. In the dozen fiscal years 1980–91, it initiated 938 criminal cases and won 794. That works out to a success rate of 84.6 per-cent.* The problem of repressing price-fixing and bid rigging, howev-er, is less a matter of the antitrust division's ability to make successful cases and more a matter of determining where violations exist and then going after them. Just about every case mentioned in this chapter had a certain serendipitous quality: it resulted from a tip, a complaint, or a lead generated by another case. It was just such a complaint from the Tennessee Valley Authority in 1959 about the receipt of identical bids on a piece of equipment that ultimately led to the exposure of wide-ranging conspiracies in electrical equipment manufacturing that had endured for years. Suppose the TVA had not complained, or William Baxter had not received that letter in 1982, or the motel manager in Virginia Beach had not protested the rise in Coca-Cola prices. Would the vio-lations still be going on, or was a complaint or tip inevitable given the degree of illegal activity in the industry? No one can possibly know.

The antitrust division spends little time worrying about generating new business or exploring new fields, since it lacks the resources to inves-tigate all the plausible complaints that it currently receives. In September 1991, there were only 267 full-time lawyers in the division—as compared with 429 in 1980—a dramatic decline attributable to budgetary constraints. (The low point was in September 1990, when the figure was 228.) Moreover, the legal staff is also concerned with investigating proposed mergers and handling a variety of civil violations. The division will not provide a breakdown of the amount of staff time spent on criminal as opposed to civil matters. But the notion of a mere 267 full-time lawyers in Washington and seven field offices (the total staff was 541, secretaries included)[21] policing all of corporate America to detect antitrust viola-tions seems quixotic, if not ludicrous—somewhat like sending in a pla-toon when a regiment is required. It is true, of course, that widely pub-licized cases can have a deterrent effect even if they do not embrace every culpable industry and every locality where violations exist. But if there are too few prosecutions, potential violators may be tempted to test their

---

* Some distortion is possible in the figures for the first and last year of the decade. In 1980 some of the recorded victories referred to cases filed before that year, and in 1991 some of the cases initiated were not resolved by the end of the year. Nonetheless, for the twelve years as a whole, the relationship between the two sets of figures can be regard-ed as roughly accurate, with the excess wins recorded for 1980 balanced in large mea-sure by the reverse situation in 1991.[20]

luck in the not unreasonable hope that they will escape the attention of the antitrust division. Even though 938 criminal cases over twelve years may seem substantial, they only average 78 a year and cannot represent more than a small fraction of the anticompetitive activity taking place. Moreover, the great bulk of the cases were in a few fields, with road building and electrical construction accounting for more than 50 percent.

An increase in staff levels would produce far more coverage. One veteran of the price-fixing wars who supports that view is Gordon Spivack, now a prominent antitrust defense lawyer who formerly served as director of operations of the antitrust division. Spivack commented at a conference in 1988, "If the antitrust division tripled its budget, they'd triple their cases. The fines they would collect and the public benefit would more than cover the increase in budget."[22]

A large increase in staff might also give the division the resources to enable it to depend less on tips. There could be more preliminary scouting of promising terrain, perhaps in industries analogous to those in which many violations have been found, in order to determine whether there is enough suspicious activity to warrant a heavy investigative effort. This is not to dispute the usefulness of tips that come in over the transom. Rather, with greater staff strength there might be some point in encouraging more and better tips by offering rewards for information that paid off, as the Internal Revenue Service has long done. A lot of fool's gold would be generated, no doubt, but there might also be some solid metal at the end of the day.

CHAPTER 4

KICKBACKS: AN OLD ART FORM

The kickback is a widespread business custom whose popularity has rarely been dampened by the inconvenient fact that it is illegal. It is popular, of course, because it is an attractive incentive for buyers to place orders with sales representatives who offer these tokens of gratitude. Its illegality has merely assured discretion in handling the transaction: cash is the preferred form of payment, and no purchasing agent in his right mind will acknowledge, except to intimates, that he is on the take.

Why is there general suspicion, then, that kickbacks are as commonplace as, say, the skimming of cash by small retail business (an offense frequently attested to by the Internal Revenue Service)? For one thing, anyone with any contact with the world of salespeople and purchasing agents continually hears about kickbacks being given and received. This is hardly proof, of course, and there is always a danger that a salesman who has failed to get an account will charge that his rival paid off the buyer. The best confirmation that kickbacks are ubiquitous comes from government investigators, who may initially stumble onto a kickback case, explore it a bit, and soon discover a vast underbrush of corruption of which they had previously been unaware.

In 1984, for example, the FBI and the U.S. attorney's office in Los Angeles began to look into charges that purchasing agents at the El Segundo plant of Hughes Aircraft were peddling subcontracts in return for kickback payments. Not only did an investigation confirm the charges, but it turned up so many additional cases that eighteen months later Robert C. Bonner, then the U.S. attorney, testified before a Senate subcommittee that "paying kickbacks on defense contracts, at least in the Southern California area, is a pervasive, long-standing practice." He estimated that "up to 50 percent of the buyers or frontline procurement personnel . . . take kickbacks in return for . . . awarding subcontracts." The loot could be immense. In a taped conversation, one buyer spoke of the good fortune of a colleague who had received $250,000 in kickbacks during one year. By the end of 1987, Bonner's office had convicted more than forty buyers, not only at Hughes Aircraft but at the Northrop Corporation, Teledyne, Rockwell International, Raytheon and Hughes Helicopters.[1]

The situation in Los Angeles was not at all unique. Early in 1988, a federal judge in Philadelphia sentenced Frank Coccia, a top Defense Department employee, to ten years in prison for running a massive kickback operation. Coccia and two of his colleagues regularly collected tribute from a wide array of clothing and textile manufacturers who specialized in supplying the military. It was a highly lucrative business. When the FBI raided Coccia's house, it found $326,000 in cash, money orders, and gold coins and another $60,000 worth of stock certificates in a safe-deposit box. He was not the only catch. By mid-1988, the U.S. attorney had obtained some twenty-five convictions. As in Los Angeles, the case had begun quite modestly, four years before, when government agents developed evidence against one errant military contractor and persuaded him to talk. One revelation remorselessly led to another.[2]

Prosecutors and private investigators have turned up kickback scandals in the most diverse fields: department stores, printing firms, supermarkets, construction companies, and all sorts of manufacturing and service establishments—indeed, wherever there is a crowd of eager sellers vying for the favor of a buyer who is empowered to make decisions. Most recipients of kickbacks are not caught, and often, when discovered, an employer will fire the offender rather than risk embarrassing publicity by referring a case for prosecution.

The kickback phenomenon falls well within the scope of this book, for it benefits the selling company that proffers the bribe. It can thus be seen as a marketing tool, and in fact is commonly regarded as such by those who employ it. It is a straightforward, if unacknowledged, way of increasing market share. At the same time, of course, a kickback victimizes the purchasing company because its employee's loyalty has been subverted and his or her judgment colored. The company may not be getting the best merchandise, though probably not something downright shoddy either, for that would endanger the purchasing agent's position. More significantly, the buyer is likely to be paying an inflated price, since wherever possible the seller will try to recoup the cost of the bribe. If passed on to the consumer, the difference in the inflated price is the economic cost of the kickback to the community as a whole.

The other possibility is that price competition is so strenuous that the briber is forced to shave profit margins to cover the kickback. There is little danger of that occurring in situations where the supplier knows in advance the kickback percentage that will be expected and tacks it on to the price; in the Los Angeles defense cases, kickbacks were set at 5 to 10 percent of the contract price. On the reasonable theory that the victimized company has been overcharged by the amount of the kick-back, courts sometimes compel restitution by the company that offered the bribe. In 1986 the owner of a Chicago printing company made a plea bargain in which he agreed to pay more than $250,000 to four customers whose purchasing agents had been bribed in that aggregate amount to throw business to the printer.[3]

The kickback is popular because of its utility and its ease. The sell-er sees it as the clinching argument, to be tried after all other persua-sive gambits have failed. To the corrupted purchasing agent, it is a perk of office, a dependable supplement to income. On neither side of the trans-action is there much of a conviction that a criminal act is occurring (although there is enough perception of risk to encourage subterfuge). In part, this is because of the belief common among white-collar offenders that the illegality of whatever they are doing is only nominal or technical, that they are not doing anything immoral (like outright thievery). They think of the transaction as victimless: "Who is hurt?" Bought buyers may conceive of themselves as merely the passive recipients of a gratuity. And they rationalize that kickbacks are commonplace in their industry, as they may well be.

But there is another element as well that explains the corrupt nexus between salesperson and buyer: the cordial atmosphere in which a sell-er seeks to envelop the relationship with the buyer. If an account is important, the sales rep pursues the buyer with an ardor limited only by the latter's sense of propriety and the former's expense account. Lunches, dinners, theater and football tickets are regarded as appropriate tokens of esteem, as are gifts at Christmas. The ingratiating seller tries to become a friend, even a confidant. Somewhere along the line may come an offer of financial assistance, perhaps to meet some pressing obligation.

The fiercer the competition among suppliers, the likelier the offer of a kickback. Similarly, the larger the number of suppliers of equal competence, the easier it is for the buyer to make a decision not based strictly on merit. Cash is the favored mode of payment in a kickback scheme, for it has obvious advantages to the recipient. But generating enough cash can be a problem for the briber, unless the company has access to large sums in the normal course of doing business. There are several solutions to this problem. One is to offer substantial gifts in kind, such as an automobile or a European vacation, both of which figured in the Los Angeles cases. A more flexible solution, giving the kickback recipient more discretion, is for the recipient to set up a shell corporation to receive kickbacks by check. Typically, the shell is no more than a letterhead or a post office box. It is wholly owned by the bribe recipient, and generally provides fictitious "consulting services," for which it bills the bribing company. The consulting fees thus become deductible business expenses to the briber, and the recipient often pays taxes on the fee income. In the Los Angeles kickback cases, a vice president at Teledyne set up such a kickback conduit with the straightforward name of "Profit Makers Enterprises."[4]

In the early 1970s, American Airlines was victimized by an elaborate scheme of this sort. The director of the sales promotion office, with the help of a corporate officer, bypassed the airline's requirement of competitive bidding and let out printing contracts to several New York firms amenable to paying kickbacks. No cash exchanged hands; instead the favored printing companies paid invoices issued by two phony companies, Visual Concepts, Ltd., and Promotional Staff, Inc., which were owned by the sales promotion manager. He then shared the proceeds with the corporate officer whose clout made the scheme possible. The latter pled guilty and was sentenced to a six-month term. The sales manager skipped town.[5] Due to the prominence of American Airlines, the case got a good deal of press attention, but it was by no means unusual in the printing industry, where bribes are common because of competitive pressures and the ability of a number of firms to handle even very elaborate printing jobs.

A variant of the technique used in the American Airlines case is for the bribing company to issue checks for seemingly legitimate corporate outlays and then convert them into cash available for kickbacks. An ingenious operation of this sort, involving laundering funds abroad, land-ed Bethlehem Steel with a $325,000 fine and a cascade of unfavorable publicity after it entered a guilty plea in 1980. The charges related not to the company's steel operations but to its ship repair division, which ran seven shipyards around the country. The money was used to bribe the employees of shipping lines to bring repair work to Bethlehem, as well as to pay bills promptly. The industry provided the classic setting for kickbacks: it was highly competitive because of surplus capacity, giving customers lots of choice. The buyer's decision could often be made capriciously.

As court documents outlined the case, the scheme involved a Swiss firm called l'Office pour le Financement du Commerce et de l'Industrie, which was in the business of selling the services of ship repair companies around the world. Bethlehem's ship repair sales office in New York would remit phony commissions to OFCI, which would deposit the checks, deduct a fee for its services, and provide cash to Bethlehem. Periodically, the head of the sales office or his secretary would fly to Switzerland, collect a suitcase full of bills and fly back to New York. In the five-year period covered by the indictment, the prosecution charged that $1 million in cash had made the journey. The government claimed that the total figure was in reality much larger, for according to its research the operation had started in 1961, long beyond the reach of the statute of limitations. Ironically, the phony commissions sent to the Swiss company actually represented fraudulent charges added to customers' ship repair bills.[6]

The initiative for a kickback does not always come from the seller. But even if the buyer suggests the payment—or indeed makes it a condition of the sale—the transaction still remains a bribe. If the scheme is detected, the seller is likely to plead extortion, but the excuse is usually legally ineffective if his sole risk was the loss of a sale and particularly if the corrupt relationship continued for some time.

Perhaps the most spectacular recent case in which the buyer created the entire kickback plan involved the International Telecommunications Satellite Organization, headquartered in Washington, D.C. Intelsat, which operates a worldwide network of communications satellites for the benefit of its 114 member countries, installed Richard R. Colino, a lawyer and longtime employee, as its new chief executive officer at the end of 1983. Four months later, in April 1984, Colino and Jose L. Alegrett, a Venezuelan who was deputy director general, launched their fraud. As later chronicled in court papers, Intelsat was in the process of building a new headquarters in Washington. The first phase was due to be completed in October 1984, and Colino promptly persuaded the board to speed up the remaining construction. He also urged that the contract not go to the construction company responsible for the first building, partly because of cost overruns, but be put out for competitive bids.

After Colino got his board to agree, deputy Alegrett sought out a real estate broker to find a construction company agreeable to a generous kickback arrangement. Following considerable negotiation, Alegrett came to a meeting of minds with the William P. Lipscomb Company of Arlington, Virginia. To the Lipscomb firm, the prospective contract represented a bonanza, for it had never built a project more than a tenth of the proposed size. Its lack of experience, however, did not deter Colino and Alegrett.

In the end, there were only two bidders for the job—Lipscomb and the builder of phase one, Gilbane Construction. To make certain of the result, Alegrett fed Lipscomb information about its rival's bid. The fine-tuning of Lipscomb's figures had its comic aspects. Initially, Lipscomb informally proposed $26 million, only to be advised to lower its bid slightly. It did so, but when Colino and Alegrett opened the bids, they found that Lipscomb's bid of $25,440,000 was still higher than its rival's. The bids had not yet been presented to Intelsat's selection committee, so Lipscomb was given another opportunity to lower its price. It proposed $25,398,000–$25,000 below Gilbane. Alegrett now feared that a $25,000 differential was too slight, in view of Gilbane's greater experience, so Lipscomb was instructed to stipulate that its bid included various electrical, heating, air conditioning and ventilation accoutrements. After it was informed of these requirements, Gilbane raised its bid to $26,348,000. Given that hefty differential, the Intelsat selection committee opted for Lipscomb. The company subsequently kicked back $2.2 million to Colino, Alegrett and two associates.

Colino and Alegrett went still further, fashioning three other kickback schemes involving the construction and financing of the headquarters project. In all, the conspirators collected $4.8 million, of which Colino's share came to $2.7 million. In August 1986, Intelsat's outside auditor, Peat, Marwick, uncovered the first evidence of wrongdoing when it came across a $1.2 million disbursement to two brokers that Colino had approved without authorization from his board of directors. One discovery led to another, and by the end of the year Colino and Alegrett were fired and the case referred to the U.S. attorney's office. Both executives pled guilty, as did the two coconspirators. Colino received a six-year prison term and was ordered to pay restitution of $850,000 to Intelsat. Alegrett repaid $1 million and was sentenced to sixteen months in prison.[7]

The Intelsat case was unusual in that it was discovered through a routine audit; most conspirators cover their tracks with greater care. Normally, the cooperation of an insider is required to crack a case, and an enormous amount of investigative time has to be expended to nail it down. The previously mentioned Philadelphia case involving the industrious Frank Coccia and the sprawling Los Angeles kickback scandal are worth examining at length for the light they shed on the problems of detecting these discreet arrangements. Both cases also provide some fascinating details about the arcane practices of the kickback specialists.

Frank Coccia, a man in his fifties, an accountant by profession, and a thirty-year federal employee when finally unmasked, had the title of deputy director of the "clothing and textile directorate" of the Defense Personnel Support Center—a major Pentagon procurement agency. Coccia nominally served under a military officer but actually ran the business on a day-to-day basis. In effect, he was the top Pentagon purchasing agent for soft goods, supervising five hundred employes in Philadelphia and buying $1.3 billion worth of uniforms, overcoats, sailor hats, ponchos, duffel bags, and whatnot. He had held the job since 1970, earned $68,500 a year, and was regarded as an exemplary employee, earning a number of awards and bonuses.

The local office of the Defense Criminal Investigative Service (DCIS) had long heard rumors that Frank Coccia was on the take, but it was never able to get any evidence. In 1983, there were also allegations of a different sort about one of Coccia's contractors—Mario D'Antonio, the head of a clothing firm called East-Wind Industries. D'Antonio was suspected of an offense known as "sample switching"—substituting pretested goods for the random sample that government inspectors had selected for quality testing. DCIS agents interviewed some of East-Wind's former employees and ultimately confirmed both charges.

Midway through its investigation, DCIS learned that the FBI had independently begun an inquiry. The two groups joined forces, each assigning four agents to the task force. Later, as leads had to be run down around the country, another dozen agents worked on the case part time. D'Antonio was eventually interviewed at his office in Trenton, New Jersey, but conceded nothing. The agents had apparently said enough to worry him, for not long afterward his lawyer informed the U.S. attorney's office that D'Antonio was ready to cooperate. "He told us that D'Antonio could give us Coccia and other people," said Frank Crocco, one of the DCIS agents present. In February 1985, D'Antonio signed a plea agreement with the U.S. attorney, in which he pledged his assistance in nailing Coccia in return for leniency for himself.

That was the break needed to crack the entire Philadelphia case. D'Antonio had done a lot of business with Coccia but not recently. The last transaction had occurred in 1981, when D'Antonio was having trouble getting Coccia's agency to settle a disputed contract claim. In return for Coccia's assistance, D'Antonio provided home mortgage loans totaling $68,000, at a below-market rate of interest, for Coccia's son and daughter-in-law—surely one of the oddest bribery instruments on record. To provide an excuse for a new meeting, D'Antonio and the agents contrived a scenario: he would tell Coccia that he needed the repayment of some of the mortgage money in order to square his books before his auditors arrived, after which he would return the money to Coccia in installments. The two men met in the parking lot of a New Jersey motel. D'Antonio wore a tape recorder, and there were also agents with videotape cameras hidden nearby. Thereafter, at periodic intervals, D'Antonio returned $2,000 at a time to Coccia, with each transaction being recorded.

These meetings generated enough incriminating evidence for the government to get a court order authorizing a wiretap of Coccia's telephone. The intercepted conversations revealed his association with a man named Leo Lamar, a former government employee who was now a consultant for a number of textile and clothing manufacturers who did business with Coccia's agency. In effect, Lamar was the go-between for customers who wanted favors. Lamar quoted the price, received the payments, deducted his share (40 or 50 percent), and passed the rest to Coccia. After investigators discovered the link between the two men, Lamar's phones were then tapped. Over a period of time, the conversations revealed his client list as well as the details of a variety of corrupt deals, and on the basis of this evidence, search warants were secured for both Coccia's and Lamar's residences. At Lamar's home, some useful documentary evidence was found, as well as $55,000 in cash. As the evidence against them mounted, Coccia and Lamar both pled guilty and furnished additional information. The U.S. attorney's office in Philadelphia characterized the case as "one of the most pervasive procurement frauds in Pentagon history." It had gone on for a ten-year period ending in 1986.

Nine government contractors were named in the indictment, though more had been involved. Basically, they approached Lamar when they wanted to rig a bid on a contract, to get an extension of a delivery date, or to resolve a dispute in their favor. Payments were not determined on a percentage basis, as in other kickback cases; Lamar merely set the price depending on the importance of the favor. According to the government, Coccia received fees ranging from $500 to $40,000, with Lamar getting an equivalent or lesser sum. (Coccia told the agents that they had a 50-50 split; Lamar said the percentages were 60-40 in Coccia's favor.) The government was never able to determine the exact dollar value of the contracts over the ten-year span, but put it at "hundreds of millions of dollars."

Coccia acknowledged receiving bribes of $331,000. In addition to his ten-year prison term, he was fined $50,000 and ordered to forfeit the $331,000 in bribe money. Lamar got three years incarceration and a $100,000 fine. Two other employes of Coccia's agency also went to jail, as did several heads of contracting firms. For his abundant cooperation, Mario D'Antonio received two years of probation.[8]

In Los Angeles, a similar story unfolded, though it had several unique wrinkles. Kickbacks had been rampant for years in the defense industry in Southern California until a voluntary informer appeared. Richard Haskell, one of the owners of a machine shop called R. H. Manufacturing Co., Ltd., had finally gotten fed up with paying kickbacks to buyers at the Electric-Optical and Data Systems Group of Hughes Aircraft. When Haskell stopped paying, orders dried up. Late in 1983, he complained to Hughes management, which called in the FBI. Haskell told his story, and in January 1984 the U.S. attorney granted him immunity from prosecution in return for his help.

Rigged up with a hidden recording device, Haskell revisited the buyers to whom he had previously sold, indicating that he had had a change of heart. He readily received orders in return for kickbacks. (The FBI furnished him with the cash.) In the end, he made cases against seven Hughes buyers and one supervisor, as well as a purchasing agent at the

Northrop Corporation. Meantime, the FBI found another cooperative subcontractor who recorded a damaging conversation with a purchasing agent at Teledyne Inc. The various tapes were so incriminating that in the end all the buyers pled guilty.

The freewheeling conversations laid out all the essentials of the scheme. While the standard kickback rate was 5 to 10 percent, the bribe was sometimes larger if the purchasing agent saw the possibility of "bumping up" the price to a higher figure than the subcontractor had originally suggested. In that case, the buyer would take a hefty percentage of the additional sum.

As Robert Brousseau, a buyer at Northrop, explained the system to Haskell, his normal kickback was "a nickel"—5 percent—on everything. But "let's say you look at a job and . . . let's say it's worth . . . a hundred bucks a part. Okay? And I come back to you and I say okay your bid was really good at a hundred bucks. I'd like to give you a hundred and seventy for it. . . . I'm going to bump it $75. . . . Okay, what I would like is 25 percent of the $75 bump. You keep the other"—a division that Brousseau regarded as "equitable." This easygoing negotiation was readily accommodated by the "competitive" bidding process that was supposed to precede the letting of contracts. Either the lowest bid was leaked to the preferred bidder or the others were asked for "courtesy bids" designed to be too high. The role of designated bidder was rotated, of course, so that everyone shared in the work.

At the time, Brousseau's department was doing work on the Stealth bomber. On May 18, 1984, in a conversation with Haskell, he provided a rare glimpse into the aspirations and psychology of the dedicated kickback seeker. The Stealth program, he suggested, was still in its infancy. "I'm 44 years old right now," he said. "I firmly intend to retire at 55. And if I just take a little piece here and a little piece there, put 'em in a shoe box and . . . bury them in the backyard . . . and don't get greedy, you know a nickel here and a nickel there. Everybody's gonna get fat and everybody's gonna be happy and at 55 I'm gonna say goodbye guys I'm gonna buy my little cabin and my fishing boat on the river."

Instead, his plans were interrupted by a three-year prison term. Fourteen other procurement officials also were convicted. The success of this initial inquiry led to the establishment of a task force in Los Angeles consisting of the FBI, the DCIS, and the IRS, operating under the code name DEFCON. Its exertions over the next two years brought the total number of individuals convicted—both bribers and bribe recipients—to more than forty.[9]

The stir created by the defense kickback cases (there were others in Louisiana, Massachusetts, Missouri, and elsewhere as well) prompted congressional hearings and a rising clamor to strengthen an old law—the Anti-Kickback Act of 1946 that covered government contractors and subcontractors. The 1946 act had obvious limitations: it dealt only with negotiated contracts and could be invoked only if a kickback was tied to a specific contract. Any other favor that a seller received, such as delayed delivery dates, was not an infraction. Penalties were limited to two years in prison and a fine of $10,000. The law clearly needed to be strengthened. Under the new Anti-Kickback Enforcement Act, passed in 1986, the maximum prison term was raised to ten years; corporations could be fined as much as $1 million and individuals as much as $250,000. Moreover, the mere offer of a bribe now constituted a crime, and payments became illegal for any preferential treatment that a seller might secure from a buyer.[10]

It is not yet clear whether the new legislation has had a deterrent effect. Since its passage, there have been a number of new kickback cases among government contractors, though none of the breadth of the Philadelphia and Los Angeles scandals. That might indicate an improvement, or merely the luck of the draw, inasmuch as prosecutors are so dependent on finding cooperative witnesses. The new federal legislation is obviously a useful tool, though, like the old law, it is limited to government contractors. The kickback phenomenon reaches into so many areas of the American economy and has become so habitual that curbing it will require aggressive action by local prosecutors as well as by top management (the final chapter elaborates on this point). A cleanup effort, however, should benefit from awareness that in this kind of crime one of the interested parties—the company victimized by a venal buyer—has even more at stake than the government.

CHAPTER 5

THE NEW GOLCONDA:
INSIDER TRADING

I n Woody Allen's 1989 film, *Crimes and Misdemeanors*, a friend tells
Allen's sister, "Oh, do I have a man for you!" To which the sister queries,
"What's the drawback?" A minor one: the fellow is in prison. But
only for a two-year term—for insider trading. And he's made a fortune.

In the 1980s, insider trading became the era's emblematic securities crime—certainly the most celebrated as well as one of the most
widespread offenses that occupied the SEC. The statistics, to a degree,
reflect the increased tempo of enforcement. During the three fiscal
years 1979–1981, the SEC charged thirty-three individuals with insider-trading violations—an average of only eleven a year. In fiscal 1987,
by contrast, sixty-six people were charged in thirty-six cases.

More significant is the fact that the cases in the 1980s were block-
busters. By the time the SEC finally caught Dennis B. Levine in 1986,
it determined that the young investment banker had "reaped" $11.6 mil-
lion in profits from scores of trades based on confidential information
over a period of years.[1] Later that year, Ivan Boesky, the best-known arbitrageur in the land, settled the SEC case against him for an astounding
$100 million[2] and thereafter received a three-year prison term after a
guilty plea.

In June 1987, the venerable firm of Kidder, Peabody squared itself with
the SEC by paying penalties of more than $25 million.[3] The firm had
benefited from a spate of insider trading and related offenses, committed by a highly placed employee, apparently without the knowledge of

topmost management. Kidder's and Boesky's penalties were eclipsed in 1989 when Drexel Burnham Lambert pled guilty to six counts of securities fraud and committed itself to paying $650 million in fines and restitution to settle both criminal charges and the SEC civil suit.[4] The magnitude of the SEC's case can be judged by the size of the forfeiture.

In the 1960s and 1970s, the relatively few cases of insider trading that the commission brought tended to be small ones, with the typical culprit not a company but an individual who traded for personal profit on the basis of "material, nonpublic" information, in the SEC's stock phrase, to which he was privy either by being an insider or by having the good fortune to be tipped off by an insider. The profits realized from such trades were generally not huge—thousands or perhaps tens of thousands of dollars to the trader alerted to the news that company X was about to launch a promising new product or announce an increase in profits or a bigger dividend.

In the 1980s, insider-trading activity boomed because it had become significantly more profitable as a consequence of two major developments: the merger and acquisition frenzy that roiled corporate America and the development of listed options. A company that was suddenly the target of a takeover bid frequently experienced a sizable jump in its stock price—30 or 40 percent or more. The reason: the price bid for the firm was always at a substantial premium over the market price—to encourage stockholders to sell—and the stock soared soon after the takeover news was flashed, if the market judged that the bid was likely to be successful. Within a day or two, the market price generally settled at perhaps 5 to 10 percent below the takeover price. At that point, the bulk of the shares had likely been bought up by arbitrageurs, who gambled on profiting from the remaining price gap when the deal finally went through.

In such a situation, anyone with advance information that a takeover offer was pending could obviously profit by buying the stock before the public announcement. Moreover, the potential profit was far greater than what might be realized by anticipating a favorable corporate development such as a dividend boost, which might advance the price 2 or 3 percent, not 30 or 40 percent or more. In addition, if the insider traded options rather than the company's stock, the profit could be eight or ten times as great.

The phenomenon of insider trading, of course, has been around since securities have been bought and sold. For a long time it was taken for granted that people who ran public companies had a huge edge over the public in trading their own stock because of their intimate private knowledge and their ability to manipulate events; that edge was only regarded as scandalous when public shareholders were outrageously fleeced. During the 1920s, insider trading certainly dismayed moralists and only confirmed cynics in their view that the stock exchanges were gambling casinos rigged against the small guy. Insider trading did not receive much public attention, however, for it was overshadowed by more flamboyant abuses such as the stock pools.

Nonetheless, the Pecora hearings sufficiently highlighted the problem so that the framers of the Securities Exchange Act of 1934 sought to scotch it. The legal curb, however, only affected corporate insiders— defined as officers, directors, and any beneficial owner of 10 percent of the stock (later reduced to 5 percent). Section 16 of the act provided that such insiders had to file with the SEC an initial report of their holdings and update any changes on a monthly basis. In addition, corporate insiders are prohibited from selling short their own company's stock or from realizing any short-term profits: any gains made on transactions within six months of purchase are subject to confiscation by the company.

The 1934 legislation, however, did not cover individuals who fail to meet the statutory definition of insiders but who are nonetheless privy to confidential corporate information. This group includes not only top-ranking corporate employees but a wide range of secretarial, clerical and accounting staff, as well as the company's outside lawyers, bankers, printers and public relations consultants. Nor did any part of the statute affect people without connection to the corporation who are the recipients of private information—"tippees" in the jargon—who are tipped off by insiders.

Not until the SEC adopted rule 10b-5 in 1942 did it have a weapon that could be employed against all misuse of inside information. Rule 10b-5 did not mention inside information as such but outlawed fraudulent practices committed by anyone—insiders or outsiders—in the buying and selling of securities. Eventually, it was applied to insider trading as well as other illegalities, on the ground that failure to disclose relevant information constituted a fraud. The rule plugged a loophole in the act, whose broad antifraud provisions otherwise applied only to brokers and dealers. Moreover, 10b-5 empowered the SEC to act against a corporation's officers and directors who were in compliance with the six-month rule but nonetheless engaged in fraud.

Insider trading, however, clearly was not a priority item for the SEC for a great many years. It was a crucial element in a report that the commission issued in 1943,[5] after an investigation of a corporation that purchased its own shares from sellers left in ignorance of relevant information; thereafter many of the legal actions in which the issue figured were private lawsuits. Not until the Cady, Roberts case in 1961, in which the SEC dealt with a stockbroker who traded on insider information, were securities lawyers jolted to full awareness of what rule 10b-5 meant.[6] Why insider trading was a low priority for the commission was not altogether clear, but it doubtless had much to do with the difficulty of discovery—especially in the precomputer era—and the lack of awareness by victims that they had been cheated.

Many people even today regard insider trading as a victimless offense. It is nothing of the sort. A truer statement is that it is a crime whose victims are nameless and faceless. "Who is hurt if I make a few bucks?" is the typical rationale of the illegal trader. The answer is simple: at any moment, there is a finite pot of profits to be made or losses to be avoided; what is taken by someone trading on nonpublic information is forfeited by others. Often the victim is the ignorant party on the other side of the transaction—who sells when the insider buys or vice versa. The victim either forfeits a potential profit or is exposed to a potential loss that would not have occurred had the insider not entered the market at that point.

It is of course impossible to know how much money is forfeited or "stolen" every year in this fashion—though the size of the loot of individual offenders is often discovered after they are caught—for the extent of undetected insider trading is unknowable. But the argument against insider trading does not depend on quantifying its economic damage. Nonetheless, a few economists argue that insider trading has its uses and should be legalized. They basically contend that if insiders were free to trade and tip off others whenever they came into possession of confidential information, the prices of securities would more rapidly reflect actual values; thus the entire stock market would become more "efficient." This might well occur, but at an enormous sacrifice of fairness.

That is the main consideration: fairness. What is the point of the vast expenditure of effort over several decades to free the securities markets of manipulative distortions if profits are usurped by traders privy to confidential information denied others? To be sure, traders and investors come to the markets armed with varying degrees of knowledge and sophistication. But the knowledge should be of a kind that everyone has a chance to acquire, even though analytic skill and experience vary widely and the abler players develop superior insights. Inside information is by definition unavailable to everybody; it is secret information, bestowed on the privileged to filch profits from the unknowing and the unwary.

If insider trading were legalized, the proverbial playing field would become so tilted as to break into two tiers: one for the professionals with access to inside dope and the other for the untutored mass of players. One can imagine the shock and disillusion and the exodus from the market. Moreover, among the professionals, bribery in the pursuit of inside information would probably become rampant.

While the SEC has traditionally taken this view, the seriousness with which it regarded insider trading only became apparent to the broader public with the celebrated Texas Gulf Sulphur case in the mid-1960s. In April 1964, Texas Gulf announced a big mineral strike—copper, zinc and silver—near Timmins, Ontario. The company's first inkling of its good fortune had come in November 1963; by the spring, laboratory analysis had confirmed it. The SEC discovered, however, that two officers of the company and one top executive had been farsighted enough to buy a bundle of Texas Gulf shares soon after the first internal communication about the find in 1963. Several other employees, officers and directors (as well as a few outsiders who had been tipped off) bought shares before the public announcement; the two officers involved waited until the day before the news release was issued to make their purchases. Once the news was out, of course, Texas Gulf stock leapt upward, to the enrichment of the happy few who were in the know.

Always the spoilsport, the SEC contended that the transactions were deceptive and thus fraudulent, giving the insiders an unfair advantage over those who sold the shares they bought. The matter was litigated at length and was widely reported in the press. The trial court knocked out the charges against several defendants, but all save one were reinstated by the appellate court, and in the end the culprits had to disgorge their profits.[7]

The Texas Gulf Sulphur case got an enormous amount of attention and established insider trading as one of the SEC's major targets. It served superbly as a horror story, for the company was prominent, the conduct of the offenders was blatant, and their profits clearly derived from their unfair edge. The case presented no ambiguity about what had happened or what was illegal. Texas Gulf, however, was not the prelude to a massive enforcement drive against insider trading comparable to the campaign the commission launched in the mid-1970s against foreign bribery and illegal political contributions by American corporations. (The SEC successfully claimed jurisdiction in this area on grounds that public companies that failed to inform shareholders of such corrupt practices—and none did—had defaulted on their legal obligation to make full disclosure of all material facts.) Instead, the SEC brought insider-trading cases as it encountered them—a trickle through the 1970s, most of them civil cases.

The law on insider trading also underwent a gradual evolution. For years, the SEC brought civil actions on the legal theory that someone trading on inside information had violated a legal obligation to disclose what he knew to the sellers. This doctrine led the SEC and the Justice Department astray in the first criminal prosecution for insider trading— the Chiarella case in New York. Vincent Chiarella was an employee of a print shop that specialized in financial documents. An enterprising sort, he took a few flyers in takeover stocks whose names he derived from documents his shop was working on. His profits were modest, but the SEC moved in on him, and in 1977 he was convicted and received a sentence of one month's incarceration and five years' probation. He appealed, and in 1980 the U.S. Supreme Court reversed his conviction on the grounds that he had no fiduciary duty to the people whose stock he bought and hence was under no obligation to inform them of what he knew. "When an allegation of fraud is based on nondisclosure, there can be no fraud absent a duty to speak," the Court declared. "We hold that a duty to disclose . . . does not arise from the mere possession of nonpublic market information."[8]

In itself, that distinction would have been a heavy blow at efforts to restrain insider trading except in the cases of corporate officers and directors as well as broker-dealers, who have clear fiduciary duties—the first group to shareholders and the second to their customers. Anyone else who came into possession of inside information—including printers, lawyers, accountants, public relations people—would be free to exploit the confidences entrusted to them. However, a dissent in the Chiarella case by Chief Justice Warren Burger outlined a "misappropriation" doctrine that readily applied to these "outsider" insiders. Burger stated that "a person who misappropriated nonpublic information has an absolute duty to disclose that information or refrain from trading." In short, if confidential information was imparted to an outsider for some legitimate corporate purpose—such as printing a document—anyone who misused that information for purposes of trading became vulnerable to prosecution for fraud. After the Chiarella case, the misappropriation theory became the standard doctrine invoked by the SEC in insider-trading cases.

A few years later, the Supreme Court added another modification in the Dirks case. Raymond Dirks was a securities analyst in New York who broke the famous Equity Funding scandal. Dirks had been informed of fraudulent practices by a former officer of Equity Funding and launched an extensive investigation that confirmed the tip. Along the way, he shared his findings with his clients, many of whom sold their stock before Equity's crisis became public and the price nosedived. In the financial community, Dirks was regarded as a hero, but the SEC went after him for violating insider-trading rules, though it only imposed a mild penalty—censure—in recognition of the public service he had performed. Dirks fought the blot on his record, and the Supreme Court ultimately held in his favor. The Court enunciated a new doctrine: inasmuch as the former Equity officer, who tipped Dirks to the problem, had realized no personal gain, he had not violated a fiduciary duty and therefore his "tippee" was not culpable.[9]

The new rule has not imposed too much of a burden on the SEC, for in most cases corporate insiders who tip off outsiders to trading opportunities do receive some personal benefit, as the spate of cases in the 1980s proved. There was, however, an odd case in Texas that pivoted on the doctrine enunciated in the Dirks case. At a track meet, a spectator overheard a corporate executive talking of a development in his company that made a rise in its stock price likely. The listener was inspired to buy the company's shares and made a substantial profit. The SEC nabbed him, but a lower court held that both parties were blameless; there was no violation of fiduciary responsibility by the corporate executive and no personal gain by him. The tip had been inadvertent; hence there was no restraint on the tippee.[10] This ruling could only encourage diligent eavesdropping in watering holes, but it made sense nonetheless.

The Winans case, which created an enormous stir, also raised a problem about what constituted insider trading. R. Foster Winans wrote a *Wall Street Journal* column, "Heard on the Street," that discussed the stock market prospects of various companies. A stockbroker bribed Winans to inform him in advance about which companies he was planning to mention, for their shares often rose in value after publication. Winans collected only a bit more than $30,000, but the broker and some of his clients profited enormously. When the scheme came to light, the newspaper fired Winans and the SEC pressed charges. There was no question about his unethical behavior, but considerable question whether he had broken the securities law. After a trial, Winans and two confederates were convicted of securities law violations as well as wire and mail fraud. The Circuit Court of Appeals upheld the convictions.[11]

Subsequently, the Supreme Court affirmed the convictions and made new law in the process. It deadlocked 4–4 on whether the securities law had been violated, thereby letting the lower court view stand, but, more significantly, unanimously held that Winans and friends were guilty of wire and mail fraud. The reasoning was that Winans had defrauded the newspaper that employed him by embezzling its intellectual property, namely, the contents and publication date of his column. The wire and mail fraud statutes could be invoked because the *Wall Street Journal* used the mails and wire communications to produce and distribute the paper.[12] Not everyone was satisfied with this ruling. In a cogent article, Professor John C. Coffee of the Columbia Law School argued that the Court had unnecessarily broadened the scope of the mail fraud statute to encompass all manner of intangible property.[13] Nonetheless, the Court has imposed a useful criminal bar against profiting from the use of what was clearly journalistic inside information.

The finespun arguments of the appellate courts have led to a lot of intellectual fun and games among securities lawyers and financial journalists trying to determine what is and what is not actionable insider trading. All sorts of hypothetical situations are outlined in which apparent insider trading may not be true insider trading. Inadvertent tipping by an insider may not result in criminal liability, but suppose an insider deliberately leaks precious information to an outsider who trades on it without the insider receiving any personal benefit in return? The Dirks decision would suggest that the insider could get away with it, but this is not necessarily the case. The personal benefit need not be monetary: the furtherance of friendship, the pleasure of eliciting gratitude, might well be regarded as a benefit to the tipper. Suppose, then, that the tipper does not trade, but passes the tip on to another, so that the final trader has no knowledge of the original source? The trader would doubtless be blameless, but the original source would still be culpable if the matter could be traced back to him.

These hypothetical situations can be fascinating, but the SEC cases since Winans that have made the headlines—even the run-of-the-mill ones—do not involve legal hairsplitting. The evidence has been so strong that most offenders plead guilty. "We've not tried to make new law since 1985," said then SEC commissioner Joseph A. Grundfest in 1989. "One reason why we're getting broad support is that all the cases we bring are black and white."[14]

One recent case that did involve legal hairsplitting—and also received considerable publicity—concerned a stockbroker named Robert Chestman. In November 1986, after the Dennis Levine and Ivan Boesky arrests had put insider trading into the headlines, Chestman traded on nonpublic information that came to him from a customer, who had received it from his wife, who in turn had gotten it from another family member; the information related to a tender offer in a large family business. Chestman was convicted but appealed. After a rare hearing before the full Second Circuit Court, in which all active judges took part, the court decided in 1991 that neither the tipper (the customer) nor the tippee (Chestman) had violated the securities law by insider trading because a fiduciary responsibility could not be inferred by a marital relationship alone. The court reversed Chestman's conviction on that ground but held that he had nonetheless violated an SEC regulation that prohibited revealing information about a pending tender offer and affirmed his conviction on that separate charge. (The customer had already made his peace with the SEC, had disgorged his profit, and paid a fine.)[15]

Insider-trading cases basically come to light in three ways: through market surveillance, through unsolicited tips, and through the daisy chain process of one admitted culprit turning in others in order to lighten a potential sentence. Market surveillance has gone on for a long time, but it has become highly effective in the last decade with the development of more sophisticated computer programs. The monitoring is undertaken by the stock exchanges and by the National Association of Securities Dealers (for their automated quotation system). All these groups track securities to detect aberrations in their individual trading patterns—sudden bulges in volume or volatile price movements, which might indicate market manipulation or insider trading. Normal parameters for volume and volatility of each security are built into the system, which enable it to kick out any divergence from the norm. An analyst will then ask the floor specialist or market maker, as well as the company concerned, about any events that might have caused the aberration. If there is not a readily available reason, such as a news break or a buy or sell recommendation by a brokerage house, the exchange or the association may open an investigation, but it can compel information only from its members, not from members' customers. If there seems to have been a violation, and if it involves people outside the exchange's or NASD's jurisdiction, the matter will be referred to the SEC's enforcement division.

At the SEC, a group of analysts and accountants headed by Richard V. Norell makes an initial assessment of the incoming data to determine if there has been a potential violation and whether it was likely to have been significant. If the answer to both questions is yes, and if his superior, an associate director of enforcement, agrees, a staff lawyer is assigned to the case. He generally begins by requesting information on a voluntary basis. If there is resistance, and if the case seems important, the commission will be asked to issue a formal order of investigation, which permits subpoenaing records and witnesses.

Every security transaction leaves a record, and it is the existence of these trading records that makes an investigation possible. They indicate the brokers on both sides of the transactions, and the brokers, in turn, have records of who placed the orders. Confirming a suspicion of insider trading involves an enormous amount of work, however. An SEC investigator will look for many things, including the manner in which orders were placed. If a broker reports that a customer rang up and said, "Buy all the stock that you can of XYZ Corporation—at market—and it must be done today," it will obviously be more significant than a customer who said, "I want to buy one of the oil stocks—you make the selection, and do it sometime this week, when the price seems best."

In examining the trading records, an investigator will first look for the most timely trades, and also for traders who might have some link with insiders at the company concerned. Names that match might indicate a family connection, or there might be a geographic cluster of trades at a crucial time, suggesting a common source of information. If a suspicious linkage shows up, the long-distance telephone records of each party may be subpoenaed; in New York City, at least, it is also possible to get records of local calls. If the suspected parties have communicated, the investigator will have a useful lever to pry loose an admission of complicity.[16]

If need be, every suspect trader will be interrogated, even in the absence of a putative link with an insider. Placing the average citizen under oath can have a sobering effect; some will tell the truth for fear of a perjury charge. But the SEC cannot count on it. The market surveillance system provides useful leads, but usually someone has to crack under the weight of circumstantial evidence in order for the agency to make the charge stick.

SEC v. W. Paul Thayer, et al.[17] was perhaps the most celebrated case to result from market surveillance, due to Thayer's prominence and the impressive (at that time) sum of $1.9 million made in illegal profits, according to the SEC's calculation. The former chief executive of LTV Corporation, Thayer was deputy secretary of defense when the SEC investigation began in 1983. He was also a board member of Anheuser-Busch and the Allied Corporation, which made him a versatile font of confidential information. Thayer did not trade for his personal account but passed information about three pending acquisitions to Billy Bob Harris, a Dallas stockbroker. Harris then bought stock for himself and several others, including a former female receptionist at LTV who, according to the criminal information filed by the government, had "a private personal relationship" with Thayer. Thayer settled with the SEC for $550,000, and Harris paid $275,000. In March 1985, both men pled guilty to a single count of obstruction of justice and two months later received four-year prison terms.[18]

Better than market surveillance is a good tip, since it obviates the need for a lot of preliminary investigation that often turns up nothing. It was an anonymous tip that led to the unmasking of Dennis Levine, who had escaped detection for seven years despite an extraordinary volume of insider trading. The story of how he was finally brought to book is worth telling in detail, for it illuminates many facets of SEC enforcement—as well as the vulnerabilities in their schemes that illegal traders tend to overlook. There is a good deal of material available on the case—masses of SEC and court documents,[19] an absorbing personal account by Levine himself, "The Inside Story of an Inside Trader," published in the May 21, 1990, issue of *Fortune*, two years after his incarceration, and an excellent book by Douglas Frantz, *Levine & Co.* I had the benefit of a dinner with Levine in a Manhattan restaurant a month after his article appeared. He was then thirty-seven, a large, voluble, expansive man, not without charm. He would not be quoted, but he seemed to be candid, appropriately apologetic about the errors of his past but hardly contrite. It was clear that his public apologia was part of his strategy to work his way back to business success. The SEC had barred him for life from the securities industry, but he could still advise clients on investment strategy and deal making and was operating a small consulting firm from his Park Avenue apartment, which he had retained through all the years since his arrest and trial.

Levine, thirty-three when caught, was a lower-middle-class product of Queens with an M.B.A. degree from a less than prestigious business school. As described by Frantz, he was powered by mammoth ambition and endowed with an awesome faith in his own astuteness. He was gregarious and could be charming, was well regarded by his superiors, and was not laughed at by his friends when he confided that his ambition was to amass $10 to $20 million and set up his own business. Early on, his chosen path to riches became insider trading. Levine also made much of his boundless ambition and the frenetic, deal-making atmosphere of Wall Street to explain his actions. "My ambition was so strong it went beyond rationality," he wrote in *Fortune.* "At each new level of success I set higher goals. . . . When I became a senior vice president, I wanted to be a managing director, and when I became a managing director, I wanted to be a client. If I was making $100,000 a year, I thought, *I can make $200,000.* And if I made $1 million, *I can make $3 million.*" He was soaring with the times: "I became a go-go guy, consumed by the high-pressure, ultra competitive world of investment banking. I was helping my clients make tens and even hundreds of millions of dollars. . . . In this unbelievable world of billions and billions of dollars, the millions I made by trading on nonpublic information seemed almost insignificant."

Levine was well positioned to amass proprietary information, for, after starting his career at a commercial bank, he worked for three investment banking houses—Smith Barney Harris Upham; Lehman Brothers Kuhn Loeb (later Shearson Lehman); and finally, Drexel Burnham Lambert, where he was hired in 1985 as a managing director; his first year's bonus came to $1 million, plus securities, according to his account. In all these places, Levine worked in the merger and acquisitions departments, perfect listening posts.

But Levine was not content with the trading opportunities that came his way in the normal course of business. His dream was to have a network of informants in investment houses and law offices all over Wall Street. Levine's piece in *Fortune* deals cursorily with these matters, but Frantz supplies a detailed account. When the game was up, Levine had benefited at one time or another from pipelines into one law firm and four investment banks, apart from his own employers. Toward the end of his deal-making career, Levine formed an alliance with arbitrageur Ivan Boesky, agreeing to supply him with tips on prospective mergers in return for fees based on a sliding scale: 5 percent of Boesky's profits on deals for which Levine was the sole informant and 1 percent in cases where Levine's information merely confirmed what Boesky had already learned.

Levine began trading on inside information in a small way in 1979 and continued uninterruptedly until September 1985. He had his losses—generally when a prospective merger or acquisition did not pan out—but they were far outweighed by profits. In its initial complaint against Levine, the SEC listed more than fifty situations beginning in 1980 from which Levine amassed profits totaling $11.6 million, plus $1 million earned in bank interest. The trades in his early years were small, but after hitting his stride Levine made as much as $2,694,422 in one killing after purchasing 150,000 shares of Nabisco prior to its takeover by R. J. Reynolds.[20]

How had he managed not to alert the computerized surveillance system? Simple. He had done all his trading through overseas banks, with the banks' names appearing on brokerage records in the United States—first Pictet & Co. in Geneva for a year or so and thereafter Bank Leu International in the Bahamas, a branch of a venerable Swiss institution. Levine depended on the bank secrecy law in the Bahamas to protect his identity in case the SEC ever got curious. Moreover, when his securities purchases grew large, he instructed the bank to split up his orders among several brokerage houses in the United States.

Levine took other precautions as well. He would place calls to his bankers from pay phones, reversing charges and using code names—he was "Mr. May" when he had an account at Pictet and "Mr. Diamond" to Bank Leu. No bank records were ever to be sent to him in the United States. On his occasional visits to Bank Leu's offices in Nassau, he might go by indirect routes, and he always paid for his tickets with cash. At the bank, he made all his withdrawals in cash. Over the years, he withdrew $1.9

million in this fashion, according to SEC documents. And, naturally, he never paid taxes on his profits.

Levine did not lie awake at night fearing detection. "I figured the odds were 1,000 to 1 against my getting caught," he wrote in *Fortune*. He had an abiding (and not unfounded) faith in his own cleverness and thought he had circumvented the SEC's surveillance system (as he had). He also thought he was amply protected by his circumspect dealings with his bank, as well by the bank secrecy law in the Bahamas. Moreover, he did not fear being turned in by one of his informants because he never gave them any hard information; they had no knowledge of specific trades or where he placed his orders. According to the *Fortune* article, he also kept his wife in total ignorance of what he was doing.

Ironically, it was one of Levine's precautions that eventually led to his undoing. As the Frantz book details, one of the additional brokerage accounts that Bank Leu opened at Levine's direction was at Merrill Lynch in New York. The broker who handled the account noticed how profitable it was and began to copy its trades in a modest way—a practice known as "piggybacking." The same broker told a friend in Merrill's Caracas office about what he was doing and kept him informed of Bank Leu's orders. The chap in Venezuela began piggybacking, as did an associate. Someone else in that office must have become aware of what was going on.

And so it came about, in May 1985, that Merrill Lynch headquarters in New York received a letter from Caracas alleging insider trading and naming the two employees involved. Merrill's enforcement office soon turned up the piggybacking in New York and the Bank Leu orders that provided the scenario. At that point, Merrill brought the matter to the attention of the enforcement division of the SEC. But a year was to elapse before the SEC was able to nab Levine.

Inevitably, it was a hard slog for the SEC. The Frantz book provides a fascinating chronicle. The SEC studied Bank Leu's trades at Merrill Lynch, going back to the opening of the account. It then queried the top brokerage houses in the United States and came up with seven others at which Bank Leu had accounts. Each brokerage house's records were checked for the time period concerned, and it then became apparent that they all had handled most of the same securities. In many cases, Bernhard Meier, an employee of Bank Leu who placed most of Levine's orders, had copied many of the trades for his own account. The SEC prepared a subpoena for the bank's records involving its trading in more than twenty securities; it also asked for Meier's personal trading records. It served the subpoena when Meier next visited New York.

Hastening back to Nassau, Meier informed his colleagues of what had happened, and they retained U.S. lawyers. When he was informed of the SEC's inquiry, Levine advised that the bank lie to its lawyers and fabricate an elaborate cover-up story, claiming that the trades had been devised by Meier, on the basis of his market analysis. It was in fact true that many of the stocks that Levine bet on were the subject of takeover rumors that had appeared in print. Meantime, the bank's lawyers negotiated with the SEC on the details of the records that were to be turned over. Theoretically, Bank Leu as a foreign entity could simply have refused to obey the SEC's subpoena. This was hazardous, however, because the bank had substantial assets in this country, which could be frozen if it disobeyed a court order to comply.

In the end, the cover-up effort collapsed because the lawyers discovered it and then persuaded the bank executives that the only solution was to try to make a deal with the SEC—trading immunity for the bank and its employees for Levine. After the SEC agreed to the deal, there was still the problem of the Bahamian bank secrecy law, for the local authorities could have imposed drastic disciplinary sanctions for a violation. But this difficulty was finessed in an imaginative way. The Bahamian attorney general decided that the bank could lift the veil from Levine because it did not have a banking relationship with him but rather a securities trading relationship, to which the law did not apply. In truth, it had both, inasmuch as Levine had maintained an interest-bearing deposit account.

Once the SEC knew Levine's identity, it had to move fast because it learned from Bank Leu that he was seeking a wire transfer of his funds—something over $10 million—to a new bank account that he had established in the Cayman Islands. The commission countered with a federal court order in New York freezing Levine's money at Bank Leu. Soon afterward, the Justice Department issued a warrant for his arrest and he surrendered. Levine's world collapsed swiftly, but he had the presence of mind, no doubt amply aided by his lawyer, to continue dealing—this time with the SEC and the office of the U.S. attorney for the Southern District of New York, Rudolph Giuliani. The weakness of Levine's position was that the SEC had a strong documentary case against him, buttressed by the detailed deposition of a top Bank Leu official who was prepared to testify in court. But even if a jury could somehow be persuaded that he had not traded on inside information, there was no doubt that he had traded extensively and profited hugely thereby—and had not paid U.S. taxes. That was a powerful fallback position for the SEC, as Gary Lynch, then SEC enforcement chief, pointed out to me long after the case was closed.[21]

Levine had a bargaining counter, however: he could reveal the identity of his confederates. In criminal cases of all types, the prosecution makes deals to bag more culprits. Mobsters will frequently not cooperate, for fear of physical reprisals. White-collar offenders, who usually have nothing to fear but hard feelings, are far more prone to betray their pals. Levine hardly received a sweetheart deal from the government, though. He had to surrender the $10.5 million in his Bank Leu account, plus another $900,000. The court gave him a two-year prison sentence; he served fifteen months and two days.

Most of the people whom Levine turned in were minor players, but he also gave the government Ivan Boesky—who in turn extended the chain of incrimination to other Wall Street eminences. When Levine had been arrested, the news created a sensation because of the magnitude of his loot, the duration of his operations, and his Drexel title of managing director (equivalent to partner). At the time, Levine was the highest-ranking Wall Street official to be arrested for insider trading. But the shock was far greater in November 1986 when Ivan Boesky's $100 million settlement with the SEC was announced.[22] For Boesky had a towering reputation, as the arbitrageur with the greatest resources and the best track record, a man known for astuteness, imagination, daring, and a phenomenal capacity to divine the success or failure of a prospective merger deal. Such at least was the legend. The raiders all knew and cultivated him; so did other arbitrageurs, who often sought his counsel and followed his lead.

When Boesky suddenly fell, it was the biggest scandal to hit Wall Street since Richard Whitney, the former president of the New York Stock Exchange, went to prison for misappropriating customers' funds. Whitney's dereliction, however, could be regarded as an isolated case of personal corruption. Boesky's disgrace not only gave the lie to his vaunted power of analysis—obviously made possible by bought information—but suggested that a deep vein of corruption infested the system. Like Levine,

Boesky soon agreed to cooperate, and before long he turned in Martin Siegel, formerly a leading takeover strategist at Kidder, Peabody, who had recently been recruited for a starring role in Drexel's mergers and acquisitions department. Siegel had fed a massive amount of information to Boesky; at one point Boesky paid him $700,000 in cash delivered in a suitcase. Siegel pled guilty to two felony counts— conspiracy to violate the securities laws and tax evasion; it also cost him $9 million to settle the SEC's civil suit. Boesky received a three-year prison term after a guilty plea to one felony count.

Siegel cooperated wholeheartedly with the government and was rewarded, three years after his guilty plea, with a prison sentence of a mere two months. Siegel implicated his old firm, Kidder, Peabody, which had profited from the insider trading for which he had been responsible; the firm's $25 million settlement with the SEC followed.[23] Siegel also implicated two of his former associates at Kidder and a well-known arbitrageur named Robert Freeman at Goldman, Sachs. For reasons that were never clear, Giuliani's minions humiliated the three men by arresting them at work and marching one of them out in handcuffs— only to quash the indictments several weeks later, promising to reinstate them in revised form but never doing so. Two years later, on the eve of his running for mayor of New York, Giuliani apologized for the error but never explained it.

Not long afterward, Freeman pled guilty to one count involving insider trading. (He received a four-month prison term and a $1 million fine in the end.) As he explained in court, Freeman had telephoned Siegel on one occasion to confirm a rumor. Siegel confirmed it. The single cryptic sentence that Siegel uttered was worth $900,000 to Freeman, Freeman's family, and Goldman, Sachs for losses avoided on a stock that he quickly sold. But the information was contraband, for Siegel was a party to the deal; he had "misappropriated" it by telling Freeman.[24] With Freeman brought to book, the U.S. attorney's office announced that it had ended its investigation of the two Kidder, Peabody employees arrested the same day as Freeman more than two years before.

But there was still a bigger catch than Siegel. Boesky also implicated Drexel Burnham Lambert and its fabled star, Michael Milken, the man responsible for the "junk bond" revolution. The SEC filed a massive complaint against Drexel in September 1988 alleging not only insider trading but the manipulation of stock prices, violation of filing requirements, fraud against customers and stock "parking"—a bogus transfer of securities to another firm while the first firm retains actual ownership. The insider-trading matters involved allegations that Drexel had profited illegally by misusing confidential information that it had received from corporate clients.[25]

After prolonged negotiations, in 1989 Drexel settled the SEC lawsuit as well as a criminal indictment by agreeing to pay fines of $300 million, to set up a fund of $350 million to compensate parties victimized by its actions, and to plead guilty to six felony counts covering some of the same allegations contained in the SEC complaint.[26] In its consent decree with the SEC, Drexel obligated itself to fire Michael Milken and his brother Lowell, to accept administrative probation for five years, to appoint three new members of its board approved by the SEC and also give the commission approval of its board chairman, general counsel and others. The company also agreed to be enjoined from committing certain specific violations of the law in the future that it neither affirmed nor denied having committed in the past—the usual formulation in such consent decrees.[27] These precautions ultimately proved unnecessary, for the firm filed for bankruptcy early in 1990 and proceeded to liquidate its business.

Not long after Drexel's plea bargain came the ninety-eight-count indictment of Michael Milken, Lowell Milken and their colleague, Bruce L. Newberg, on charges that covered much the same ground as in the SEC complaint against Drexel.[28] The major difference was that the various counts were wrapped in the embrace of a RICO (Racketeer Influenced and Corrupt Organization) conspiracy, which vastly inflated the seriousness of the securities and mail fraud allegations and enabled the prosecution to ask for an enormous penalty, involving triple damages—the sum of $1.8 billion, no less.

The use of the RICO law in a case of securities fraud was controversial, to put it mildly; it is a subject to which we revert in the last chapter. The government contended that the Milken operation demonstrated a pattern of pervasive racketeering. One will never know whether a jury would have accepted the ambitious sweep of the indictment, for in the spring of 1990, after loudly proclaiming his innocence for two years and vowing to fight every charge, Michael Milken suddenly agreed to a plea bargain. He pled guilty to six criminal counts, among them conspiracy to violate securities law, market manipulation, aiding a client's effort to evade taxes, and defrauding the customers of a Drexel investment fund, but not insider trading—all of which subjected him to a potential twenty-eight years in prison (which no one expected him to get). He also agreed to part with $600 million—$200 million in criminal fines and penalties and $400 million in a disgorgement fund to be available for civil claims against him.[29]

Late in November 1990, after an extended court hearing on the government's and the defense's massive sentencing memorandums, Judge Kimba Wood finally imposed a ten-year prison term on Milken. It was longer than most observers had expected and elicited considerable criticism as well as support. My own view is that the sentence was not excessive. No one believed that Milken would serve the full period: he would get time off for good behavior and be eligible for parole even earlier. (The new sentencing guidelines, which limit a judge's discretion, do not allow parole, but Milken is not affected because his crimes occurred prior to November 1987.) The most important consideration, however, is the seriousness of the offenses to which he pled guilty. Market manipulation, abetting tax evasion, and defrauding customers are neither trifling nor "technical" offenses, as his defenders have suggested, though the means used to effect these deceptions were indeed highly technical and discreet; these were not street crimes or even high-powered con games. The customers felt no pain nor were even aware of their victimization but were fleeced nonetheless. Moreover, any defendant who agrees to plead guilty to a reduced number of criminal counts is likely to be guilty of a greater number, though perhaps fewer than those charged. A plea agreement, after all, is a bargain between a defendant who wants to limit his exposure and a prosecutor who prefers a limited victory to risking all at a trial. In imposing sentence, a judge is entitled to consider the entire pattern of a defendant's behavior, which is the whole point of the elaborate sentencing memorandums and court hearings, a procedure that the Supreme Court has long held to be valid. In sentencing Milken, Judge Wood stressed the deterrent impact on others of a stiff sentence. She also pointed out that Milken had a chance to get his term reduced if he finally cooperated with the authorities, which meant providing information that might lead to further prosecutions. Both motives underscore the fairness of the sentence.

This elaborate chain of events began, as we have seen, with Dennis Levine, who was tripped up by an anonymous tip arriving in the mail.

A fiction writer fabricating such events would be hard put to establish the verisimilitude of the scenario. Now that it has occurred, both Congress and the SEC have been amply persuaded of the utility of tips and have sought to encourage them. A provision of the Insider Trading and Securities Fraud Enforcement Act of 1988 authorizes the SEC to provide bounties to informants whose tips lead to the apprehension of violators. The rewards can range up to 10 percent of the penalties imposed—often likely to be a substantial sum, given the outcome of several recent cases. The helpful folks in Caracas, for example, could have received over $1 million had the law been in effect in 1985. The 1988 act also allows the SEC to file a civil suit in federal court for a penalty up to three times the profit made (or loss avoided) by insider trading and increases criminal fines to a maximum of $1 million (from $100,000) and prison terms to a maximum of ten years (from five).

The incentives to tipsters and the severe penalties threatening violators should logically act as powerful deterrents. So should the highly publicized cases made by the SEC over the last several years. Gary Lynch, after heading SEC enforcement during four years of zealous pursuit, believes that the incidence of insider trading has markedly fallen.[30] But by the nature of the crime, no proof one way or the other is possible.

All those scalps that the SEC has hung out to dry may well have had the intended exemplary effect. When Dennis Levine started his scheme in 1979, no one using a foreign bank as a shield had been netted by the SEC. Most of the illegal traders who had been caught were unsophisticated small fry. But now that several powerful figures have been toppled, the calculation of the odds of detection must have shifted among all those risk weighers on Wall Street. Anyone is a fool who believes that if only two people share a secret both are safe, on the reasoning that one person's word will be no more credible than another's in court. Trading records leave a long trail, telephone records can be circumstantially probative, a private conversation can be taped—as Boesky apparently taped some of his associates before his ruin was publicly known.

But there is no reason to believe that this awareness and this caution will be permanent. Memories fade as enforcement drives fade. Old and new players will revert to old tricks if the SEC's efforts slacken. Nearly a year elapsed before the commission promulgated rules for the new bounty system. It then prepared a pamphlet on the program and distributed two thousand copies; it is available to anyone who asks[31]—all of which hardly constitutes an aggressive publicity campaign. In response to a Freedom of Information Act request, the SEC declared in January 1991 that it had received seven applications for bounties, approved one, rejected another, and had five pending. It is time that the agency made full use of one of the best weapons available. One detects in many quarters a shying away from the energetic recruitment of informants—for fear of creating a dismal, Big Brother atmosphere. But the fear itself is unrealistic. It is a subject to which we will return.

CHAPTER 6

TAX EVASION: SKIMMING AND

OTHER PLOYS

To anyone attracted to crime, tax evasion has great appeal, whether the prospective beneficiary is a corporation or an individual. It can generate large sums of money. It may require only one simple, repetitive scheme that will endure for years rather than the variety of conspiracies involved in, say, bid rigging or price-fixing. Moreover, if done deftly enough, tax evasion stands an excellent chance of escaping detection, for it is less vulnerable to being spotted by computerized surveillance systems than insider trading or market manipulation.

Above all else, there is the enormous money that can be earned with little effort. Take the instructive case of Joseph H. Prettyman, Jr., an enterprising businessman who, starting in 1978, expanded a single restaurant in Dewey Beach, Delaware, into a complex of four restaurants, retail shops and a convention center, doing an annual volume of business of $5 million. In nine years, according to the government's calculation, Prettyman squirreled away $2.4 million in cash, thereby avoiding both corporate and personal income tax of about half that sum.

Prettyman's technique is called skimming. Restaurants and retail shops inevitably generate a huge volume of cash, making it easy, in closely held establishments, to skim off the top—a hallowed term that originated before dairies had learned to homogenize milk. The process for Prettyman was simplicity itself. Each day he instructed his secretary how much money was to be separated from the company's cash receipts and deposited in a safe under the floor of his office closet. The rest of the money was dispatched to the Rehoboth Beach branch of the Wilmington Trust

Company. The bookkeeper kept two sets of books—one recording the company's true receipts and the other reflecting the receipts less the sums skimmed. The phony figures were then used by the company's controller to prepare its corporate income tax return.

According to the IRS's calculations, Prettyman consistently skimmed about 7 percent of cash receipts from 1983 to the time of his arrest in 1987—$292,000 in 1983, $306,000 in 1984, $318,000 in 1985, $350,000 in 1986, $371,000 in 1987. The government had exact data for those years, but it charged that Prettyman had started the skimming operation back in 1979, his second year in business. On the assumption that he had held to a 7 percent average skim, the government estimated his overall take came to some $2.4 million. Not all that money went directly into his pocket. He dipped into the floor safe to pay some of his suppliers in cash—presumably those who were keen on trimming their own tax bills. He also devised an incentive cash bonus plan for his top executives, thoughtfully not reporting the sums involved on the employees' W-2 forms. Prettyman's secretary also received a $5,000 annual cash bonus—"hush money," he once explained, to keep her quiet by implicating her in illegality should she ever have been tempted to blow the whistle.

Prettyman could feel safe because all the individuals who knew about the scheme benefited from it. Moreover, he was careful not to skim too much and thus attract the IRS's attention if the company's books were audited. A 7 percent skim still left the company's profits-to-sales ratio in line with the national average, as Prettyman once remarked in a conversation that he did not know was being recorded. Such statistical conformity meant one of two things: either Prettyman's business was more profitable than most such operations or the national figures themselves reflected a good deal of hidden income.

However sophisticated his setup, Prettyman was still too trusting—and was finally undone as the result of an IRS undercover operation. Introduced to someone interested in buying his business, Prettyman showed surprising candor, outlining his skimming exploits to prove that the business was worth more than its stated profits would indicate. He apparently never suspected that the prospective buyer was working for the IRS and wearing a hidden recording device. Prettyman incriminated himself with happy abandon. Before long, the feds were back with a search warrant and soon had the records to back up his statements. In 1988, Prettyman pled guilty to one count of conspiracy to defraud the government and another of filing a false income tax return. The federal prosecutor, David C. Weiss, called Prettyman "the most serious tax offender in the history of tax prosecutions in this district." The judge gave him six years— a stiff sentence in a tax case.[1]

In IRS jargon, Prettyman's crime involved "underreporting" receipts in order to evade taxes. A lot of it goes on, according to IRS studies. In 1987, small corporations like Prettyman's (defined as those with assets of less than $10 million) were estimated by the IRS to have underpaid their taxes by $2.5 billion as a result of not reporting all their receipts. That same year, "nonfarm proprietors," such as small shopkeepers, reduced their taxes by $16.6 billion by failing to report $86 billion in revenue.[2]

Tax evasion is unique among business crimes in that the government agency concerned with repressing it makes diligent efforts to measure it. The IRS is in a position to do this, whereas the antitrust division of the Justice Department is not, because of the millionfold tax returns that it routinely collects and because it is empowered to audit the books of any taxpaying entity in the land, or of anybody who is not paying taxes but the IRS has good reason to believe should be doing so. Thus, every few years, the IRS goes through an elaborate exercise to determine what it calls the "gross income tax gap" for individuals and corporations— defined as "the amount of income tax owed for a given year, but not voluntarily paid." Voluntarily means without such enforcement action as audit examination, criminal investigation, and dunning.

The IRS has been making these estimates for every three years since 1973, producing a bewildering array of numbers that are worth sorting out. For 1987, the year for which the most detailed figures are available, the service estimates that the gross tax gap was $84.9 billion. Of that total, $63.5 billion represented "noncompliance" by individual taxpayers and $21.4 billion by corporations.[3] The latter figure, however, does not represent the entire tax gap of the business sector, for the corporate figure excludes sole proprietorships, partnerships, and so-called subchapter S corporations, which are not subject to corporate tax. According to the IRS's estimates, these various groups had a tax gap of $27.6 billion in 1987, attributable solely to unreported receipts.[4] Adding that number to the noncompliance figure for the corporate sector produces a grand total of $49 billion for the gross tax gap of the nonfarm business community.

Some of those billions were later captured as a result of IRS enforcement activity. Of the $84.9 billion gross tax gap figure for all taxpayers, the IRS estimated that it would eventually recover $21.9 billion—$8.3 billion from corporations and $13.8 billion from individual partnerships and other taxpayers. That still left an enormous net tax gap, any reduction of which would make a helpful dent in the national debt.[5]

It should be stressed that neither the gross nor the net tax gap is synonymous with tax evasion. For the felony of tax evasion to occur, there must be specific intent to defraud the government. Honest error, even negligence, is not the same as criminal intent, though it may well result in a civil penalty as well as the payment of interest on back taxes. Nonetheless, the size of the business tax gap suggests the magnitude of tax evasion. For 1987, "nonfarm proprietors" reported $89.3 billion in income and failed to report $86 billion, as previously noted. No one believes that more than a trifling proportion of the latter figure represents honest error, given the ease with which cash-heavy business can cheat.[6]

The IRS's estimate of the tax gap is painstakingly put together from several sources.[7] For individual taxpayers, sole proprietorships, partnerships and small corporations, the basic source is the Taxpayer Compliance Measurement Program (TCMP), a detailed audit of fifty thousand randomly selected taxpayer returns. A TCMP audit is a far more probing, not to say nitpicking, examination than the audits to which millions of taxpayers are routinely put each year, with a much higher level of proof required—even to the extent of producing a marriage certificate to validate the claim to a joint tax return. In estimating the tax gap, the IRS's general technique is to determine the shortfalls in the tax calculations on the TCMP returns, then project them, with appropriate weighting, over the entire universe represented by the fifty thousand sample returns.

The overstatement of deductions is easier to detect than the underreporting of income, since it is relatively simple to spot lack of proof for a claimed deduction. In some cases, unreported income can be discovered through third-party information returns—W-2's and 1099's—that reveal larger receipts than the taxpayer reported. The real problem comes from unreported cash income, in situations where the payer does not file information returns. In this area, the IRS relies on a variety of survey data to estimate the shortfall in unreported cash income; it does the same thing to calculate the income of people who do not file returns.

In the case of large corporations—defined as those with assets of $10 million or over—there is no TCMP data and the IRS must extrapolate from the information found on its normal corporate audits to develop its gross tax gap estimates. The largest corporations (with assets of $250 million or more) are audited at least every two years and often once a year, in as detailed a fashion as in any TCMP audit.

Between 1973 and 1987, the estimated gross tax gap tripled from $28.4 billion, largely reflecting increased economic activity as well as inflation. But while the tax gap has grown, the extent to which taxpayers submit accurate tax returns has not greatly changed, as is apparent from what the IRS calls the voluntary compliance rate. This has remained remarkably stable. Starting at a figure of 83.7 percent in 1973, the VCR has twice dipped below 82 percent but was back to 83.2 percent in 1987. Over the same period, the rate for individuals was a bit higher than the average (reflecting automatic withholding of tax on wages and salaries), while the rate for corporations was a little lower, hovering below 82 percent until 1987, when it increased to 82.5 percent (probably attributable to the lowering of tax rates that year). Although the situation has not worsened over the years, rates in that range certainly indicate a huge potential margin for improvement.[8]

According to the the tax gap figures, there is far more noncompliance by unincorporated businesses and small corporations than by large corporations, which accounted for a gap of $15.8 billion in 1987.[9] The difference is largely accounted for by the greater ease of cheating in small firms, the widespread use of cash, the relative lack of controls, and the difficulties the IRS and state tax authorities have in policing a vast universe of small units. The IRS would have the same problem with individual taxpayers were it not for withholding.

Large corporations have much greater difficulty cheating than small ones do, since they maintain all sorts of internal financial controls, designed to prevent misuse of funds, embezzlement, as well as pilferage by lower-level employees. These same controls, monitored by layers of management and outside auditors, make it harder to evade taxes. Moreover, the larger the corporation, the more likely it is to have IRS examiners hovering over its shoulder. When large companies or some of their employees attempt to cheat, the schemes generally need to be more sophisticated than in the case of small business.

Although small companies will indulge in other evasive tricks, skimming cash is by far the most popular form of cheating. Many of them are flooded with cash in the normal course of business, particularly in the vast field of retail trade, which consisted of no fewer than 1,441,200 establishments in 1986, the great majority of them modest in size. Despite the growth of supermarkets, there were still 131,100 grocery stores in 1986, 19,900 retail bakeries, 141,800 clothing stores, 289,500 eating places, 50,200 bars.[10] In these enterprises, the use of credit cards notwithstanding, cash has never lost its popularity, which means endless temptation for the small shopkeeper. Moreover, the retail atmosphere is markedly casual in its attitude toward the tax law. Some employees are eager to work "off the books" all or part of the time, to evade personal income tax or, in the case of Social Security recipients, to keep their reported incomes under the allowable level until the age of seventy, when the cap on earned income is lifted. Suppliers also frequently ask to be paid in cash.

Moreover, technically it is easy to skim. In some stores with several cash registers, one might be run without recording its transactions on a master register, or several might go unrecorded for a couple of hours before closing.[11] More important, as any sophisticated tax evader knows, is a symmetrical alignment of the skimming with the financial profile of the enterprise. To avoid arousing an examiner's suspicions during a tax audit, the reduced volume of sales resulting from pocketing cash must be kept in line with the payroll of the firm and the volume of its purchases. If the skim is too large, the sales volume will seem too low to support the enterprise. The solution is a coordinated slenderizing of the firm, with some employees working off the books and some payments to suppliers made in cash. In so doing, the firm saves not only on income tax, but on Social Security and sales taxes. It may also save on payroll costs, paying some employees less because they are relieved of income tax.

At the same time, the employer has to make sure that the overall slimming of the operation does not go too far, that all the scaled-down figures on the books are plausible in light of the rent, the visible volume of traffic in the store, and the number of employees that a visitor sees. All of which makes possible a cash skim of as much as 10 or 15 percent, depending on the nature of the business. An auto dealership, for example, could normally skim very little, for most purchases are paid for by check or by installment credit. On the other hand, many restaurants could get away with more than the 7 percent that Joseph Prettyman managed.

For companies that find it impossible to skim cash, claiming false or inflated deductions is a popular alternative. To deduct fictitious items from income, after all, is an equally effective way to reduce taxable profits. One of the most elaborate of such schemes in recent years was an invoice-selling operation in New York City that involved some two hundred companies and at least $136 million in phony deductions. Prosecuted by the U.S. attorney in Manhattan in 1987, it resulted in the conviction and imprisonment of the three individuals who ran the scam and the conviction of more than a dozen businessmen who also benefited from it.[12]

Why the trade in invoices? An invoice is a bill requesting payment for an itemized list of goods and services. It constitutes evidence that a sale has taken place, and when the buyer in turn remits a check in payment, that act is taken as proof positive that the transaction has been completed. To the buyer, the purchase constitutes part of the cost of doing business. The higher the costs, the lower are the profits; the lower the profits, the less tax the firm has to pay. All this is elementary. But contemplate the financial alchemy wrought if there is an invoice for goods sold and a check issued in payment even though no goods have changed hands. Suppose that the seller who issued the invoice returns 90 percent of the buyer's payment in cash. The buyer does not record the cash on the books, of course. Instead, the cost of the goods presumably purchased will be recorded, thereby reducing the tax liability. For that, the buyer has paid 10 percent of the face value of the invoice. The tax saving, naturally, is far greater—a few years ago it could have been more than 50 percent of the sum invoiced (calculated at the top federal rate of 46 percent, plus state tax, before the Tax Reform Act of 1986 went into effect). All that for a 10 percent commission taken by the clever folks who sold the invoice.

That in essence was the scam perpetrated in New York for several years by Schnejer Zalman Gurary, a septuagenarian Hasidic rabbi (without congregation), his son-in-law, Rabbi Nochum Sternberg, and his daughter, Esther Sternberg. Gurary was what the government called the "decision maker" in the scheme, setting the level of commissions—which ranged from 5 to 15 percent—and supervising the entire operation. Sternberg was one of the salesmen and deliverymen of the cash. His wife Esther, who worked out of their Brooklyn home, kept the books, prepared the invoices, and communicated with the bookkeepers of the invoice buyers. Gurary employed two other salesmen and cash dispensers—Al Mayo and Irving Katcher, both veterans of New York's garment district.

Mayo and Katcher would call on people they knew, soliciting business in the same manner that they might peddle yard goods. The pitch was straightforward: Mayo would tout the great utility of an invoice, which could be "used as a purchase, a regular purchase, and [the customer] could pocket the money and use it for whatever purposes" he desired. Mayo also tried to expand his customer list beyond the garment center and managed to recruit a structural steel firm. Gurary was initially reluctant, for none of his invoice-selling companies handled steel products. The problem was solved by deleting the word "textile" in the company name and slicing off the bottom of the invoice, which contained a standard warning about the flammability of textiles.

Apparently game for anything, Mayo also sold some "charitable contributions" at Gurary's urging. This scheme, described at the trial but not part of the indictment, in effect involved the sale of receipts. An individual would contribute, say, a $10,000 check to a bona fide charity, receive a receipt for the gift and $9,000 in cash. The contributor would then have a $10,000 charitable deduction for his or her income tax return, which could be documented in an audit with both the receipt and canceled check. The charity, of course, would only receive $1,000, but without Gurary's enterprise, it might have received nothing. Gurary himself did not profit from the deal; this was apparently one of his "pro bono" activities.

Gurary and associates dealt exclusively in paper. As the prosecutors put it, "During the duration of the invoice-purchasing scheme, the defendants and the Zalga companies had no goods for sale, no delivery trucks, no warehouses to store textiles, no employees, and no showroom to display goods." They operated out of one nondescript office or another, but they did go about their scheme in a meticulous way. They usually provided a bill of lading as well as an invoice to a customer as additional proof that a shipment had been made. Each invoice-issuing company was more than a mere letterhead, in fact, a legally incorporated entity. Over the years, Gurary set up thirty-six separate companies, often containing the name Zalga—Zalga International Enterprises, Inc., Zalga Marengo Textiles, Inc., Zalga Metropolitan Textiles Corp., and so on. Each corporation stayed in existence only for a year or two, but scrupulously filed corporate tax returns, showing only minimal profit or none at all.

The point of this charade was to protect Gurary's customers. If an invoice purchaser was audited by the IRS, the auditor might grow curious about one of the Zalga companies and call for its tax records. If there were none, the auditor might become suspicious. Indeed, the entire scheme was shaped with a view to escaping detection by the IRS. During an audit, a revenue agent would routinely check to see that the purchases journal was backed up by invoices and canceled checks and that the checks were endorsed on the back with the same name as the payee on the front. The fake bills of lading served as further documentation of a legitimate purchase.

The checks that Gurary received from his customers were duly deposited into Zalga accounts at four different New York City banks; there was a total of fifty-five separate bank accounts for thirty-six corporations between May 1978 and May 1986; each account was active for a year to two and a half years, and Gurary was a signatory on fifty-three of them. From 1979 to 1986, checks were deposited into those accounts, mostly from companies in the garment center, adding up to $136,551,973. The data the government obtained from the banks were incomplete, however; subsequent examination of the records of the invoice-purchasing companies indicated that the banks had given the government information that covered only 75 percent of the checks deposited in the Zalga accounts.

That explained a substantial discrepancy revealed in the investigation: the government discovered that Gurary and friends sent some $158 million to Switzerland over the seven-year period. There was nothing subterranean about the transfer. Several times a week, the Gurary corporations would debit one of their accounts anywhere from a few thousand dollars to $500,000 and obtain a check from the bank. One of the group would then take the check to another New York bank—Republic or Lloyd's Bank International—and have the funds wired to a Swiss bank account.

The government never discovered who owned these Swiss accounts. Some might have belonged to Gurary and the Sternbergs, but by no means all, for their gross profit on each sale was limited to the commission. Nor did the government ever discover the origin of all the cash that Gurary disbursed to his customers. It certainly was not generated from cashing the checks made out to the Zalga companies, for the bulk of those funds—the $158 million—was transferred to Switzerland. Nor was there any evidence that Gurary had arranged an airlift of cash via suitcase from Switzerland to the United States.

The likeliest possibility, suggested by one of the government prosecutors, is that Gurary was laundering cash skimmed by other business firms, perhaps for a commission of 1 or 2 percent. In other words, a customer would come to Gurary with a bag full of cash and turn it over to him to be transferred to Switzerland; Gurary would take the cash to service his invoice-buying customers and use their deposited checks to make the wire transfer to a Swiss bank. This is a plausible scenario, suggesting an inflow of $400,000 to $500,000 a week. But the government could not know for sure, since Gurary and the Sternbergs never cooperated.

For the defendants, the scheme was clearly a bonanza. Just on the basis of the minimum of $136 million in sold invoices, an average commission of 10 percent would have brought Gurary $13.6 million over a seven-year period, subtracting minimal office costs and the modest commissions he paid Mayo and Katcher; the prosecutors calculated that Mayo made $30,000 to $40,000 a year and Katcher $40,000 over the entire period. As for Gurary's customers, they not only saved on corporate income tax, but on personal income tax as well on the sums that might have had to be paid out in dividends. Some of the cash went for corporate purposes—for kickbacks and payments to vendors who also wanted cash. One of Gurary's customers, for example, testified that each year he would pay employees cash bonuses totaling $25,000 to $30,000 and use $60,000 to $70,000 for kickbacks to buyers. What money was left was split between the business partners. Over the years, the company bought $700,000 worth of invoices.

Despite the involvement of more than two hundred companies in purchasing invoices, the IRS never discovered the scheme. It seemed foolproof. True, the secret was shared by many, but every participant cheated on taxes and thus had a motive for discretion. Finally, however, someone did develop a motive to talk—and it was one of Gurary's biggest customers, a man named Irving Feiner, whose women's apparel company, Ahead-by-A-Length, had purchased $26 million in phony invoices from Gurary and the Sternbergs between April 1980 and January 1983. Feiner had been recruited by Al Mayo but later dealt directly with the Sternbergs and Gurary. By 1981, Feiner was apparently inundated with cash and had Gurary furnish him with bearer bonds instead. Such bonds, of course, had the virtue of paying interest while being as anonymous as cash.

By 1985, however, Feiner was in deep trouble with the law, being sued by two banks for obtaining loans with phony collateral and facing the risk of prosecution by the feds on the same matters. In negotiation with the U.S. attorney's office, Feiner offered a bigger prize as part of a deal—he gave them Gurary. Without lifting a finger, the government now had nabbed the biggest invoice-selling scheme ever to come to light in New York.

Developing the case took a lot of work. It proceeded in classic fashion. The government first moved in on Al Mayo, whom Feiner had implicated, and won his cooperation by giving him immunity. Irving Katcher made the same deal. Gurary was then arrested, a fact duly noted in the newspapers. The news gave Mayo an excuse to call his old customers, without telling them, of course, that the conversation was being recorded. As soon as they heard Mayo on the line, the customers were voluble in expressing their consternation and proceeded to make the kind of damaging admissions that only amateur criminals would utter over the telephone. Katcher also had some conversations of the same sort.

The government then approached the hapless businessmen and played the incriminating tapes for their lawyers. One by one, the businessmen agreed to cooperate in return for some mitigation of penalty. (In the end, they all got probation.) Fifteen testified against Gurary and the Sternbergs, as did salesmen Mayo and Katcher. During the six-week trial, the goverment introduced a mountain of bank records and other physical evidence. The three defendants were convicted. Gurary received a three-year prison sentence and fines totaling $2 million. Between them, the Sternbergs were fined $1 million; the husband received a prison term of 18 months and the wife, 120 days. In 1988, the Second Circuit Court of Appeals upheld the conviction, and the U.S. Supreme Court subsequently refused to accept the case.

Corporate schemes to evade taxes tend to have the complexity of the Gurary operation, for they are designed to withstand the scrutiny of a tax audit. One ploy that is hard to detect involves phony trading losses, which are then used to offset profits and thus lower taxes. It has figured in a number of tax shelter cases and constituted a large element in the indictment a few years ago of Marc Rich, the celebrated New York commodities trader who escaped the clutches of the IRS and the Justice Department by fleeing in 1983 to Switzerland, where he still flourishes.

Many of the dodges also have the same repetitive quality as the Gurary scheme. In one of the most famous criminal tax cases on record, involving the Fruehauf Corporation, then a well-known manufacturer of truck trailers, the company's chairman and president were found guilty in 1974 of conspiring to evade payment of federal excise taxes for a period of ten years.[13] The scam worked this way: the IRS allowed a manufacturer to calculate the 10 percent excise tax on the wholesale price it charged distributors. The manufacturer remitted the tax to the IRS, and the distributor in turn passed it along to retail customers. To gain a competitive edge by reducing the size of the tax, Fruehauf contrived a clever gimmick—shaving the wholesale price by billing the distributor separately for advertising, sales, and financing services, which had formerly been included in the overall sales price. On the ancillary services, Fruehauf now charged no tax.

The IRS ultimately discovered the dodge. The company's guilt was underscored by the fact that it never altered the percentage cut from its sales price, although the services provided to its distributors changed over the years. Sitting without a jury, a judge convicted the company and its two top officers in 1974 and sentenced each to a six-month jail term. Later, after their appeals were lost, the judge changed his mind and instead gave them probation and community service. The defendants always insisted that their scheme was legitimate. Final sentence was not imposed until 1979. Today, given the harsher attitude toward white-collar criminals, the two executives would doubtless have been required to serve time in prison.

Evasion of gasoline excise tax has been a major problem for the IRS in recent years, particularly in the Northeast. Until a few years ago, the federal excise tax was collected at the wholesale level. Special licenses, exempting wholesalers from paying the tax, were available for merchants who wished to trade the gasoline among themselves. The first unlicensed wholesaler who bought the gas was supposed to pay the excise tax and be reimbursed by the retailers who bought from him. The scheme involved long chains of faked trades between companies, making it difficult to determine who was responsible for the tax; when the IRS was finally ready to pounce, the company had often disappeared. Disentangling the chain of collapsed companies proved to be a daunting task, but the IRS made a number of successful criminal cases in New York State. The problem has since been partially solved by changing the law and collecting the excise tax when gasoline is sold at a storage terminal. But the IRS now has to contend with phony sales within the terminal.[14]

Some of the culprits in these cases pocketed millions that should have gone to taxes, but their names meant nothing to the casual reader of the press accounts. Not so in the case of the sales tax frauds that made headlines in New York in the mid-1980s. Some of the toniest stores in town were involved, such as the jewelers Cartier, Van Cleef and Arpels, and Bulgari, which were charged with routinely helping their customers evade sales taxes on expensive items. The stores' motive was to gain a competitive edge, for the combined New York state and city taxes came to 8.25 percent, which amounts to a hefty sum on a $1,000 or $10,000 purchase. The technique was the same in each case. The customer was urged to carry the merchandise home and to provide an out-of-state address to which the store would send an empty box, inasmuch as no sales tax was required on an out-of-state delivery. Some furriers were involved in the same scam. The tax sleuths found that the stores' records indicated that a one- or two-pound box would be sent to New Jersey or Connecticut whereas the average fur coat weighed seven pounds.

The little game was no intermittent occurrence. The city's investigation indicated that two-thirds of Cartier's sales went untaxed, rising to 90 percent of its sales over $10,000. In the end, the three jewelry establishments pled guilty, as did several other companies. Cartier had to pay $2.2 million—$1.2 million in unpaid taxes, $647,000 in interest, and $336,000 in penalties and fines.[15]

The IRS is hardly defenseless against tax evasion, but it is far from realizing its full potential. In part, this is because of the agency's multiple roles—education, collection, enforcement—in part because of the funding constraints under which it operates. The service has a large educational task in explaining a deplorably complex tax code so that citizens can follow the instructions and pay the taxes due. The IRS presents itself as the taxpayer's friend, offering a slew of helpful publications and responding to telephone inquiries—though often providing misinformation (23 percent of the time, according to the agency's figures for fiscal 1990) both because of the complexity of the tax code and the lack of adequate training of the employees on the line.

At the same time, the agency must show itself to be a stern watch-dog, guarding the sanctity of the tax code, quick to intervene if the tax-payer makes an honest error and to undertake a criminal investigation if illegal acts are suspected. The agency wants to enforce without seem-ing to intimidate—a perfectly reasonable goal but one that leads to less enforcement than is possible far short of the IRS being transformed into Big Brother. And, of course, there is never enough money for a full enforce-ment effort.

The shortcomings of the enforcement effort are nowhere more apparent than in the field of tax audits. The audit of an individual, part-nership, or corporate return is an essential enforcement tool that car-ries no implication of criminality, though on occasion an audit might reveal grounds for suspecting criminal acts, in which case the matter is referred to the IRS's Division of Criminal Investigation, with the tax-payer being so informed. Despite the audit's key role, however, the sad fact is that audit coverage—the percentage of tax returns subjected to the process—has been steadily declining over the years. The IRS cal-culates the coverage rate by comparing the number of audits in any one year with the tax returns filed for the previous year. This involves an unknowable element of imprecision for any particular year because the audits conducted in, say, 1991 involved tax returns not only for 1990 but for prior years as well. Nonetheless, the IRS believes that report-ing the statistics consistently in this fashion over many years gives a real-istic sense of changes in audit coverage.

In fiscal 1991 the coverage rate for all individual tax returns (of which there were 112,304,900 filed for the previous year) was 1 percent—up from 0.8 percent in 1990 but down from 1.03 percent in 1988 and 2.11 percent in 1979. In many cases, the audit coverage of the larger returns had fallen almost as dramatically, and in some instances more so. The coverage rate in fiscal 1991 was 3.63 percent for the tax returns of sole proprietors reporting total gross receipts of $100,000 or more on their schedule C's. By contrast, the figure was 5.8 percent in 1981, the first year the IRS provided a gross receipts breakdown. Similarly, only 2.36 percent of all corporations were audited in 1991, as contrasted with 7.4 percent in 1979 and 8.01 percent in 1978.[16]

The overall decline began in 1980 and continued remorselessly thereafter. The major reason was budgetary restrictions, the inability or unwillingness of the administration to spend more money to keep up the audit ratio as the volume of returns increased. To be sure, the IRS budget did rise, but not enough to compensate for inflation, the ever-greater number of tax returns, and the heightened complexity of the auditor's task due to the many changes in the Internal Revenue Code. In addition, in the mid- and late 1980s, the IRS embarked on an admirable drive against abusive tax shelters, thereby diverting a sizable chunk of the audit force from its routine tasks. In the last few years, the audit "mix" was altered to cover more corporate returns as compared to individual ones—another estimable initiative that also took its toll of the coverage ratios. In fiscal 1989, money grew so tight (on top of everything else, there was a mandatory pay increase for federal workers) that the IRS had to impose a hiring freeze, leading to a decline in the number of auditors and criminal investigators.

The great irony is that IRS audits bring in more money than they cost. In fiscal 1991, the entire IRS examination and appeals process cost $2.065 billion; additional taxes and penalties recommended by the examiners came to $32.28 billion. (The term recommended is used because the dispute goes up on appeal if the taxpayer does not agree with the auditor's decision.)[17] Most of the money is eventually paid. Years ago, the view in the IRS was that the return from audits would double if the audit investment doubled. Currently, the experts' view is more cautious; a substantial rise is anticipated, but hardly a doubling.

No administration has proposed that the IRS double its audit coverage, despite the certainty of a big revenue gain. In January 1990, however, the Bush administration finally proposed a modest increase in audits in fiscal 1991 that would begin to reverse the long decline. The administration's budget proposal had the IRS adding about 2,400 positions and spending $135 million more in the audit field, including postal queries of taxpayers about single items, all of which it estimated would produce increased revenue of $537 million in fiscal 1991 and $5.7 billion over five years. The overall audit rate would rise to 1.3 percent in fiscal 1991—still a long distance, of course, from the 1979 rate.[18] In the end, the Congress gave the IRS almost all the money it asked for, and the audit rate went to 1 percent; there are no present plans to push it higher. In addition, during 1991 the IRS began to concentrate more attention on the largest corporations through its "coordinated examination program," picking up more than $1.7 billion in additional revenue.[19]

The purpose of auditing returns, obviously, is not only to increase revenue but to deter the larcenously inclined. But what is the deterrent effect if the owners of a subchapter S corporation know that they have but 1 chance in 117 of being audited, as was the case in 1991, or if a sole proprietor with receipts over $25,000 but less than $100,000 realizes that his chances of being scrutinized in depth is less than 1 in 50? He might be tempted, instead, to play "audit roulette"—to take outrageous liberties with the law because of the high probability of being overlooked. This situation has existed for a long time and inevitably leads to the suspicion that everybody—the IRS, the Congress, the administration—prefers the present level of relatively relaxed enforcement to one where the number of audits would be increased to the point where they ceased to be cost-effective. Everybody, it would seem, fears the screams of enraged taxpayers.

The ambivalent attitude of the IRS is even more vividly on display in the strange manner in which it handles its program of rewarding informers, a program that was in place long before the income tax law was enacted in 1913. Section 7623 of the Internal Revenue Code authorizes the IRS to pay rewards for information that uncovers a tax violation and enables the service to collect back taxes and penalties. The informant is paid on a sliding scale, depending on the value of his information and the amount recovered; the percentages range from 10 percent down to 0.5 percent, and in no case can be more than $100,000.

Substantial sums are involved. In fiscal 1991, for example, the IRS received 9,907 claims for rewards, approved 732, paid $1,549,730 in reward money, and recovered $58,370,096 in taxes, fines and penalties. The rewards paid in one year do not necessarily pertain to the moneys recovered that year, for the rewards always lag the recoveries; hence it is impossible to work out a meaningful average ratio between the two. From fiscal 1985 through 1991, the highest reward total was $2,764,634 in 1990 and the highest recovery total was $258,372,000 in 1986.[20]

Despite the lack of a symmetrical match between rewards and recoveries, it is clear that the program has a big payoff. Moreover, the raw figures give no notion of the importance of a case that may have resulted from a tip. It is remarkable, under the circumstances, that the IRS does nothing to publicize the reward program. It is never mentioned in the many publications the service offers the taxpaying public, nor even in its annual report, which describes a multitude of activities. All the IRS issues about rewards, to anyone who asks, is a skimpy, two-page flyer narrow enough to fit into a number-10 envelope.[21] And the press office will provide reward statistics to an inquiring journalist.

The subject of rewards and informers seems to embarrass the service. "The organization has for a long time had a policy of not publicizing the reward program," says Inar Morics, the assistant commissioner for criminal investigation. He fears that actively promoting the program would smack of a "police state mentality," adding, "It would be viewed more as a 'turn in your neighbor' rather than a 'turn in the bad guys' kind of a thing."[22]

There is little doubt that informing, when it involves friends and associates, is despicable on a personal level. The disgruntled employee or vengeful ex-lover who betrays a tax cheat is hardly a role model for the young. Yet every police agency is dependent on inside information, and almost all of them pay for it. Despite the IRS's disdain for advertising, its willingness to pay gets mentioned here and there in newspaper and magazine stories, so the tips keep rolling in.

Yet clearly more could be accomplished with the program, if only as a tool for deterrence, without threatening the liberties of Americans or promoting paranoia about talebearing neighbors. The service need not advertise the program in the media, but could reasonably mention it in IRS publications. The copious IRS instruction booklet for form 1040 has an abbreviated contents list on the front cover. Suppose a line was added reading "Rewards for Information," with a page reference to a boxed paragraph or two on the inside that spelled out the details of the program and indicated that the service was not interested in rumors or suspicion but hard information about apparent violations. What would be the result? An influx of more tips, no doubt, most probably worthless, but in addition many a potential cheat who read the notice might get a sudden jolt of apprehension that stayed his hand.

It could be argued that there is no need to promote the reward program because the Division of Criminal Investigation (CI), which Morics heads, is already stretched so thin that it cannot handle all the cases referred to it. The division has only 2,800 special agents, that is, professional investigators; the rest of the 4,000 or so employees are primarily clerks and secretaries. The agents are highly trained and marvelously skilled at disentangling paper trails and turning up indirect evidence of hidden income; many of them are also adept at undercover work. But despite all the attention focused on the tax gap in recent years, CI has not grown. It had approximately the same number of special agents a dozen years ago. Meantime, however, the celebrated "war on drugs" and the new preoccupation with money laundering absorb the energies of more than 1,100 special agents, leaving only 1,600 spread over 63 district offices to deal with general tax enforcement. During fiscal 1991, the division spent $275,886,000, only a 10.7 percent rise over 1988—considerably less than the rise in inflation over the four fiscal years.

Fiscal constraint seriously limits what CI can do. The division initiates investigations in response to informants' tips, leads from prior investigations, and referrals from the examination division, which audits taxpayer returns. Morics's people then sift the cases and select the most promising to pursue. "We can't possibly work all of the tax evasion that is alleged and brought to our attention," he says, "so we try to get coverage"—by which he means a reasonable geographic distribution of cases that is also representative of different industries and occupations. CI's aim, he explains, is "to work a deterrent effect, so that people will figure, 'Hey, if I do this, I'm going to get caught.'" But however artful the selection of cases—cases that make headlines are obviously the best deterrent—the result is that a good deal of tax evasion goes uninvestigated and thus unpunished.

The limitation on resources also means that CI never undertakes a broad industry investigation without some very specific targets in mind. At any one time it can maintain only forty to fifty undercover operations throughout the country (there was a total of 201 during fiscal 1991). I asked Morics if a productive assault on the tax gap might not come from an open-ended undercover effort in some retail field with a large cash turnover—in just about any big city. Suppose he sent in undercover agents, posing as waiters, to work in several restaurants, for example. Morics found merit in the idea if only he had the staff for it, but saw no point in diverting resources to an open-ended investigation when CI could not handle all the specific leads that came its way. He readily agreed that he could use more resources—what criminal investigator would not agree?—but quickly added, "How much is enough I do not know." The essential question was what level of enforcement is necessary for adequate deterrence. Morics could not say. But present staff and financing are clearly not enough.[23]

Early in January 1990, Fred T. Goldberg, then commissioner of internal revenue, told the *Wall Street Journal*, "If we had more people and better trained people, we'd raise a lot more money." Hardly a startling observation, but he added a kicker; asked how much more money, he replied, "You need 40 billion? You got it."[24]

But no administration within memory, no congressional faction, and certainly no group of embattled citizens has campaigned to put the IRS on full rations. Almost every agency of the federal government is dependent on the IRS's ability to raise revenue, yet the service has no constituency urging it to do a better job. Lobbying on tax matters largely takes the form of seeking tax breaks for a particular industry or trying to ward off increases in excise taxes on an industry's products. But nobody lobbies to pay for those parochial tax breaks by enabling the IRS to collect more revenue through greater efficiency.

The last thing most people want is a more efficient IRS. Paying taxes has never been one of the more attractive duties of citizenship, to put it mildly; the only time people lobby for taxes is to shift the burden onto someone else. Moreover, taxes have rarely been in such bad odor as during the last decade, thanks largely to the zeal with which two presidents preached the doctrine of permanent tax reduction. The resentment against taxes is naturally directed at the tax collector as well. One might cynically speculate that as a consequence many citizens harbor felonious fantasies about tax evasion, which they are incapable of putting into effect but which lead them to identify with tax cheats. More likely, the public fears that a stronger IRS might turn up minor errors and arguable delinquencies in their tax returns and make life miserable for them.

On the other hand, there is palpable outrage when a notorious tax evader, such as New York hotelier Leona Helmsley, is put on trial; people vent their anger against what they perceive to be an inequitable system that exacts every last dollar from the modest wage earner, whose paycheck gets deducted automatically, while giving the rich many opportunities to cheat. In the end, it is probably that ambivalence in public attitudes that has hobbled the IRS. The politics of the situation suggests that anyone trying to strengthen the IRS has to exploit the public's hostility toward big-time tax cheats.

CHAPTER 7

THE MANY GUISES OF FRAUD

As a business crime, fraud has wide appeal. By definition its essential ingredient is the use of deception to effect a theft of some sort. Such deception is a component of several of the crimes that we have already dealt with—tax evasion, which defrauds the government; insider trading, which defrauds the investing public; kickbacks, which defraud the recipient's employer; price-fixing and bid-rigging schemes, which defraud the customer. But apart from these specific, highly individuated crimes, there is also a more general category of corporate fraud that covers a variety of deceptive practices in pursuit of profit. Consumer fraud is but one form of such delinquency; another was the esoteric check-overdrafting scheme that the venerable brokerage firm of E. F. Hutton perfected a few years ago to victimize its banks.

There are business firms, of course, whose sole purpose is to devise frauds and thereby separate suckers from their money as expeditiously as possible. Con men of all sorts, credit card fraudsters, boiler room operators who peddle worthless securities by telephone have long been with us. They are a pernicious breed, who engage Better Business Bureaus and state attorneys general in a thousand skirmishes a week, but they are beyond our scope. Here we are concerned solely with legitimate and often otherwise estimable businesses, whose occasional fraudulent practices hardly constitute their raison d'etre. Many of these companies are household names—among them Beech-Nut, Chrysler, Hertz, and, among defense contractors, such prominent manufacturers as General Electric, Litton, Northrop, and the Loral Corporation.

However varied, their frauds have several characteristics in common. They have tended to be of long duration, with each of them involving the complicity of many individuals; once discovered, they are readily documented by a substantial residue of paper—all of which rules out error or happenstance as an explanation for the offenses. Instead, each of the scams has been carefully planned and supervised, at least on the middle-management level and sometimes higher. But prosecutors can rarely prove that the topmost levels of a corporation have been involved, whatever their private suspicions.

A few frauds are so esoteric that some of the participants may not grasp the full import of their actions. In the early 1980s, for example, E. F. Hutton was engaged in a massive overdraft scheme in which it surreptitiously stole millions of dollars from its banks. Scores of branch offices and scores of banks were involved, and it is quite possible that many lower-level employees had no notion of what they were up to. (The people running the operation were far more sophisticated, however.) The essence of the scam was to write checks against deposited but uncollected funds in such a fashion as to overdraw Hutton's accounts without the banks knowing what was going on. Overdrafts in themselves are of course legal, so long as the banks are aware of them; they often charge interest. But Hutton's massive, criss-crossing check-writing scheme was pure trickery.

In the criminal charges to which Hutton pled guilty, the Justice Department alleged 2,000 counts of fraud between July 1, 1980, and February 28, 1982, involving aggregate drawings "well in excess of $1 billion" against uncollected funds. Even with the briefest of loans, sums of that magnitude meant millions in interest savings. This was aggressive "cash management" with a vengeance, and it was properly held to be illegal. Hutton paid a $2 million fine, consented to an injunction, and agreed to pay restitution to the banks. The Justice Department, however, was widely criticized for not prosecuting any of the individuals involved.[1]

The sheer brazenness of the scams is striking. For the better part of a decade, ending in mid-1986, the Hertz Corporation systematically cheated its customers and their insurance companies by foisting on them phony and inflated bills for automobile repairs. In all, about 110,000 customers and third parties were victimized to the tune of $15.7 million. All thirteen zones of Hertz's Rent a Car division were involved in the scam.

A variety of deceptive techniques were employed. Typically, Hertz received a volume discount on the work it gave body repair shops but would charge the customer the nondiscounted price, which the company referred to as the "retail price." In some cases, Hertz employees would forge the dollar figure on the vehicle repair form that it sent the customer;

in other cases, employees would make up new, phony forms and forge the names of appraisers. Bills were further inflated by charges for the days the damaged car presumably could not be rented, even though Hertz usually had a supply of unrented cars during the period.

In some parts of the country, Hertz would put repair jobs out to bid, generally asking submissions from three shops. It would accept the lowest bid but routinely submit the highest to the customer for payment. It also played another game that internally it called "enhancements"—inflating legitimate bills to include repairs that had not been made or replacement parts that had not been purchased. In other cases, where the damage was small, no repairs at all would be made, but Hertz would send the customer a bill listing fictitious payments to a nonexistent repair shop.

At least fifty people in various Hertz offices were involved in the scheme and many more knew about it, but it went undetected for years until a disaffected former employee in the Boston office, angry over being fired, decided to blow the whistle. She got in touch with the Boston representative of the Insurance Crime Prevention Institute, a private agency, which started an inquiry and found enough incriminating evidence to take to the U.S. attorney in the Eastern District of New York, in Brooklyn, one of the many areas in which the fraud was going on. The case was put in the hands of Jonny J. Frank, an assistant U.S. attorney who heads a unit known as special prosecutions. Frank's investigation stretched over many months and involved subpoenaing Hertz repair records from offices around the country and interviewing lower-level employees. The documents, plus the knowledge (furnished by the informant) of the code words used internally by Hertz, enabled Frank to build a crushing case against the company. In the end, Hertz agreed to plead guilty to charges of fraudulent billing during the period from January 1978 through the summer of 1985; it paid a fine of $6.85 million and pledged restitution to its billed customers of $13.7 million. The latter figure was an estimate of Hertz's illegal revenue that the accounting firm of Coopers & Lybrand calculated from a detailed analysis of a random sample of Hertz's vehicle repair files.

Why had the fraud endured so long? In part because of its own momentum; no one was moved to betray it. "The employees did not assume that what they were doing was criminal," says Frank. As is often the case with corporate delinquency, long practice seemed to validate questionable behavior. New employees simply did what they were told. Many employees rationalized their conduct on the grounds that Hertz was simply trying to compensate for losses suffered when customers defaulted on their obligations. And some employees, who had qualms, understandably feared losing their jobs if they complained. None of the employees, of course, benefited personally from the scheme—another characteristic of such frauds that tends to appease consciences. The fraud naturally made department managers look efficient, but Frank and his colleagues were persuaded that the top executives of the corporation had no idea of what was going on in the so-called accident control departments around the country. If those on the highest levels of authority had exercised some elementary foresight, they could have prevented a public relations disaster.[2]

In Chrysler's celebrated odometer case, the executive suite was again guiltless in a widespread consumer fraud. It had started out innocently enough. Chrysler had long run a test-drive program for new cars, in which plant executives drove a sampling of new models for brief periods, often on personal business. To disguise the fact that the car had been driven around town, its odometer would be detached beforehand; thus it appeared to be virginal when it finally appeared in the retailer's showroom. That constituted the fraud; Chrysler was selling as new a car that to some degree was used.

Worse deceptions have been committed, to be sure, but deception it surely was. It went on for decades until 1986, when a number of Chrysler employees were stopped for speeding in Missouri. They imprudently informed the complaining officers that their cars lacked odometers as well as speedometers, a needless admission that led to a lengthy investigation by the state of Missouri, the U.S. attorney in St. Louis, and U.S. postal inspectors. Out of it emerged a lengthy, sixteen-count indictment that charged that the fraud started way back in 1929 and specifically involved unrecorded mileage on sixty thousand cars driven by Chrysler employees and subsequently sold to the public between July 1985 and December 1986. With the odometer removed, obviously nobody could tell how many miles had been covered, but the indictment stated that each car involved was driven between one and five days.

In some instances, however, employees disregarded instructions from plant managers to disconnect odometers, and the cars registered what was regarded as an excessive amount of mileage—upward of 100 and in one case more than 418 miles. But all was not lost; new odometers were simply installed to replace the old. No effort was made to hide the practice from plant employees, for it was the subject of several memos from quality control managers and others in various Chrysler plants. In one instance, a teamster strike prevented the trucking of cars between a Chrysler assembly plant in St. Louis and an outside body shop, which installed special roofs, in St. Charles, Missouri. To get the cars outfitted, Chrysler instructed the contractor to drive them back and forth with disconnected odometers.

The indictment was perhaps even more damning in describing more than forty instances in which cars in the test program were involved in accidents. In some cases, the damage was severe, but the vehicles were routinely repaired and sent on to retailers for sale as new.[3]

When the indictment hit the headlines in June 1987, Chrysler's first response was a feeble denial that anything "illegal or improper" had been done. But, faced with a cascade of negative publicity, within a week chief executive Lee Iacocca sought to make amends by announcing at a news conference that the odometer cover-up was "just dumb" and that selling damaged cars as new "went beyond dumb and reached all the way out to stupid." He pleaded personal ignorance of what had gone on, and offered to make amends by extending warranties another 20,000 miles on cars whose odometers had been tampered with or replaced. He also offered new cars to customers who had purchased damaged ones.[4]

Later in the year, the company agreed to a deal with the prosecutors in which it pled nolo contendere to all sixteen counts in the indictment and settled civil suits with forty-one states and other parties by agreeing to spend at least $16,375,000 to compensate victimized customers. Each would receive at least $500. A nolo plea, of course, results as automatically in a conviction as does a guilty plea, but it may sound better to refuse to contest a charge rather than flatly admit guilt. That was small solace in a public relations debacle whose financial impact was hard to calculate.[5]

The by now famous Beech-Nut apple juice case was unusual both for the personal involvement of the company's top executives and the unambiguousness of their motives: to fatten or at least safeguard the bottom line. Chief executive Niels L. Hoyvald had inherited rather than initiated the fraud; his culpability lay in continuing it and covering it up. The Beech-Nut Nutrition Company, since 1979 a subsidiary of the Swiss corporation Nestle S.A., had long been one of the nation's three leading manufacturers of baby food. Apple juice was one of its most popular items; the company labeled it as 100 percent pure, unsweetened fruit juice. In 1977, Beech-Nut changed the supplier of the apple juice concentrate from which it made its bottled product, thereby reducing the cost of the ingredient—as much as fifty cents to a dollar per gallon.

In October 1978, Dr. Jerome LiCari, Beech-Nut's director of research and development, became suspicious that the concentrate was adulterated and eventually was convinced on the basis of laboratory tests that it consisted largely of sugar syrup, with little or no apple juice. There was no health issue; the stuff was safe to drink, but babies were not getting what their parents thought they were buying. Alarmed, LiCari made repeated efforts to get Beech-Nut to drop its supplier, but he was never able to persuade the vice president of operations, John F. Lavery, who seems to have regarded LiCari as a naive pest. Lavery was no innocent in the affair. Mislabeling apparently did not trouble him, and he lectured LiCari on what was at stake financially.

In LiCari, Beech-Nut had an irrepressible whistle-blower. Not every company is so blessed, but Beech-Nut gained no benefit, for LiCari elicited only scorn from top executives. In April 1981, Niels Hoyvald, who had joined the company the previous year, became president. LiCari and others in the company informed him of the adulteration problem, but he refused to act. LiCari resigned his post.

Then, in June 1982, Hoyvald and Lavery were suddenly confronted with a crisis. A detective working for the Processed Apple Institute, who had been quietly investigating Beech-Nut's supplier, told Lavery that Beech-Nut was about to be sued for using adulterated concentrate. Lavery was finally moved to fire his supplier and ordered that the stash of concentrate in the company's plant in upstate New York be destroyed or returned. But that still left the company with a major problem: a huge inventory of bottled apple juice. Fearing seizure by New York State authorities, who had already begun an investigation, Hoyvald ordered that the hoard be shipped by trailer truck—in the dead of night, as it happened—from the plant in Canajoharie, New York, to a warehouse in Secaucus, New Jersey.

By this time Hoyvald was also aware that the Food and Drug Administration was looking for the suspect merchandise, and he managed to ship almost all of it to Puerto Rico before the FDA could find it. Soon afterward, he hurriedly shipped the apple juice stocks in the company's San Jose, California, plant to the Dominican Republic, offering discounts of up to 50 percent to get rid of it. With most of the junk out of the country, Hoyvald then agreed to the FDA's demand for a recall of the bottles that remained on store shelves. All these exertions saved the company a loss of $3.5 million—"conservatively estimated," as one of its lawyers put it—at the price of its reputation, however, once the scandal broke.

The FDA and the Justice Department were not to be put off. After a protracted investigation, a 470-count indictment came down in 1986 against the company, Hoyvald, Lavery, and four other individuals involved in supplying, labeling, and shipping the mislabeled product. The counts involved charges of conspiracy, mail fraud, and violations of the Food, Drug and Cosmetics Act, with 449 of the counts—each specifying a shipment—relating to the latter. A year later, the company negotiated a plea bargain, in which it agreed to plead guilty to 215 counts and was fined $2 million—the largest fine ever imposed under the Food, Drug and Cosmetics Act, according to the Justice Department.

The four other individuals involved also pled guilty. Hoyvald and Lavery stood trial. They were both convicted, but Hoyvald's conviction was later reversed by the Court of Appeals, on the grounds that he was tried in the wrong federal district court. Hoyvald's second trial resulted in a hung jury, but he subsequently pled guilty in a deal to avoid jail. Instead he received five years' probation, six months' community service, and a fine of $100,000. Lavery was sentenced to a year and a day in prison, as well as a $100,000 fine. Both men, on paid leave during trial with the company picking up their legal costs, lost their jobs.[6]

Why had they done it? In a long and detailed account of the case in the New York Times Magazine in 1988, James Traub wrote that "the Beech-Nut baby-food scandal is a case study in the warping effects of blind corporate loyalty."[7] True enough, but the blindness was not merely to ethical considerations, as the phrase suggested, but to several other qualities as well that top executives ought to possess, especially prudence and imagination. What was remarkable in the whole sad chronicle was the unwavering persistence of Lavery and Hoyvald in continuing the fraud long after suspicion had been aroused. Both men showed an incredible lack of judgment in thinking that they could indefinitely avoid detection. All that they could focus on, apparently, was the expense of ending the adulteration. They could hardly have made a cost-benefit calculation, since the penalty for exposure in terms of damaged reputations was far more than fines or even a jail term.

To a large extent, the mainsprings of fraud can be described as a perversion of all the incentives that propel a well-functioning capitalist system. The drive to best the competition, to win the contract, to reduce costs, to maximize profits are supposed, in an ideal world, to promote efficiency and the most rational use of resources. They often achieve these ends, but the same competitive drive unfortunately produces an impulse to cheat, particularly in an environment where cheating is easy, the stakes are high, and the odds against getting caught are favorable. These generalizations apply to all forms of corporate fraud, of course, but they seem particularly relevant to a crime that makes headlines almost every day of the week—fraud in defense procurement—to which we turn in the next chapter.

CHAPTER 8

DEFENSE PROCUREMENT FRAUD: A CORPORATE WAY OF LIFE

E arly in 1986, a poll of public attitudes toward the defense industry was conducted for President Reagan's Commission on Defense
Management, popularly known as the Packard Commission,
after its chairman, industrialist and former top Pentagon official David
Packard. The poll's findings could not have been more disquieting. "On
average, the public believes almost half the defense budget is lost to waste
and fraud," the commission reported. Moreover, "Americans believe that
fraud . . . accounts for as much loss in defense dollars as waste. . . ."
Arithmetically, that would have meant that almost 25 percent of the
defense budget—then running at about $300 billion a year—was dis-
sipated by fraud, 25 percent by waste. The problem was nowhere near
that big, the commission hastened to assure us: "While fraud constitutes
a serious problem, it is not as extensive or costly as many Americans
believe."[1]

No doubt about that, yet it is easy to understand why the American
public has an exaggerated impression of misbehavior by defense
contractors. While they don't make off illicitly with 25 percent of
our defense dollars—indeed, no estimate is possible of the overall cost
of fraud—major defense contractors have been guilty of criminal offenses that can hardly be regarded as peccadilloes: defrauding the government by misstating contract costs, falsifying test results, collusive
bidding, gaining illegal access to classified documents, and employing consultants who bribe Defense Department officials, among
other transgressions.

Moreover, the offending companies include some of the most cele-brated names in American industry, which guarantees widespread pub-licity, as it should. Look at a roster of wrongdoing during 1989 and 1990 alone: The Northrop Corporation pled guilty to falsifying test results on parts it made for the cruise missile and the Harrier jet. It was fined $17 million.[2] Teledyne Industries Inc. admitted its guilt in a conspiracy to defraud the United States and to commit bribery, wire fraud, and the fil-ing of false statements, among other offenses, and paid fines and civil penalties of $4,363,742.[3] In a case that arose from the same investiga-tion, the Loral Corporation pled guilty to conspiracy to defraud the United States and other misdeeds, paying $5,770,000 to make amends.[4]

In a linked series of cases in 1989–90, the Boeing Corporation, General Electric's RCA unit, the Grumman Corporation, Hughes Aircraft, a unit of General Motors, and Raytheon Co. all pled guilty to illegally trafficking in classified Pentagon documents.[5] In 1990 as well the Emerson Electric Company parted with some $14 million to settle charges, to which it pled guilty, of bilking the Pentagon by inflating con-tract costs.[6] Fairchild Industries' VSI unit pled guilty to phonying test results for fifteen years, for which it paid a $2.5 million fine, $1 million in costs, and $14.5 million in a civil settlement.[7] For the same offense, E-Systems, Inc., another large defense contractor, pled guilty and relin-quished $4.6 million; it had falsified test results on field radios shipped to the army.[8]

All these offenders were major players in the defense business. In 1989, General Electric was the nation's third-largest defense contractor, General Motors was the fifth-largest, Boeing was the eighth-largest, Grumman the eleventh, Northrop the thirtieth, Loral the thirty-sixth in rank.[9] Of the hundred largest defense contractors, at least thirteen corporations (or their subsidiaries) were convicted of procurement fraud during the twenty-month period ending August 31, 1990.[10] It can be argued, on the one hand, that fully eighty-seven had clean records; nonetheless, a crime rate of 13 percent among the goliaths of defense production indi-cates a problem that is neither fortuitous nor trifling. Smaller compa-nies were by no means blameless; their crimes account for a large chunk of the statistics. In fiscal 1987, there were 180 convictions for procure-ment fraud; 295 in fiscal 1989; and 393 in fiscal 1991.[11] And these statistics represented only the most promising cases that came to the atten-tion of defense auditors and investigators. Many instances of fraud in which the evidence was less compelling resulted in civil suits and settlements. And, as with all crime, many frauds obviously escape detection.

There is little mystery about what makes the Pentagon peculiarly vulnerable to fraud. Its vast purchases—contract authorizations (over $25,000) totaled $137.7 billion in fiscal 1991[12]—are quite unlike the procurement efforts of private business or even much of the rest of government. In the private sector most purchases are of stock items at fixed prices, although long-term contracts may have escalator clauses to cover inflationary increases. To be sure, the Department of Defense buys many off-the-shelf items just as private companies do—motor vehicles, clothing, food, office supplies, and thousands of other items, all of which rarely give rise to scandals (the huge bribery case at the Philadelphia military clothing depot, dealt with in Chapter 3, being a notable exception). With stock items, the DOD can solicit competitive bids and compare price and quality from various suppliers; it then signs fixed-price contracts.

The situation is entirely different with weapons, communications, and computer systems, which constitute an enormous part of the Pentagon's budget. With these complex programs, the accent is on innovation, new and untested designs, and often new technologies. When these programs are in the research and development or prototype production phases, there is no easy way to determine a reasonable or a fair price—for the price depends on a forecast of future costs, a notoriously difficult and imprecise exercise when a new fighting machine or a new piece of scientific gear is being developed. Moreover, the DOD is by necessity the sole buyer—at least until the device is perfected, when it might be sold abroad as well. And given the huge development and production costs, it also depends heavily on sole-source suppliers. As a monopsony dealing with monopolies, the Pentagon cannot rely on the discipline of the marketplace and is therefore in a highly exposed bargaining position. To prevent itself from being gouged, the DOD relies on a complicated negotiating process, plus audits, to ensure that the manufacturer's stated or anticipated costs are not inflated and that its profits are held to reasonable levels. What is a reasonable profit is by definition arbitrary and is determined, subject to negotiations, by complex guidelines dealing with risk, the cost of money, and other factors.

The DOD uses a bewildering variety of contracts to accommodate the many contingencies encountered in research and development and in production work. There are cost-plus-fixed-fee contracts, cost-plus-award-fee contracts, cost-plus-incentive-fee contracts, cost-sharing contracts. (Fee is the term used for profit.) Incentive-fee contracts, in turn, are of two major types—fixed-price incentive contracts and cost reimbursement. In all these arrangements, the name of the game is flexible pricing. As a government publication explaining the Federal Acquisition Contract system[13] points out, "Complex requirements . . . usually result in greater risk assumption by the government. This is especially true for complex research and development contracts, when performance uncertainties or the likelihood of changes makes it difficult to estimate performance costs in advance. As a requirement recurs or as quantity production begins, the cost risk should shift to the contractor, and a fixed price contract should be considered."[14] But even with fixed-price contracts, the ultimate price can fluctuate as the supplier encounters variable costs of labor and materials during the course of the job; in some cases adjustments are made as a result of changes in actual costs, in others on the basis of changes in cost indexes alone.

Flexible pricing can promote efficiency if the government negotiates skillfully. In the case of incentive contracts, if a contractor comes in under the target price, it benefits by way of an increased fee. But the system can also result in erroneous or purposeful shifting of charges from one cost account or contract to another as well as overcharging for labor or materials—in a word, cheating. The publication warns government contractors that "before agreeing on a contract type other than firm fixed-price, the contracting officer shall ensure that the contractor's accounting system will permit timely development of all necessary cost data in the form required by the proposed contract type. This factor may be critical when the contract type requires price revision while performance is in progress."[15]

To keep contractors honest, the government has long had a truth in negotiations law,[16] revised in 1986 and 1987, which requires that contractors bring to the negotiating table cost and pricing data that they certify to be accurate, complete, and current; the government has the right to examine the contractors' books to make sure. Any data later found to be falsely represented open the contractor to a charge of defective pricing, allowing the government to recoup overcharges. If such defective pricing is intentional, it is by definition fraudulent.

Typically, there is fierce competition when the Pentagon solicits bids for the design contract for a new piece of equipment, since the company that wins the design job generally ends up as the sole-source supplier for years to come. In their competitive zeal, some companies intentionally underbid on design as well as on production contracts, if the latter are put out to bid—with the hope of recouping their losses legally or illegally. The legal way is to try to recapture cost overruns by filing claims for reimbursement with the claims boards of the various military services. The illegal way is quicker, though not without hazard: devising schemes to inflate costs in some circumstances or to disguise cost overruns in various ways, thereby increasing revenues, or to skimp on product testing or substitute cheaper components; there are many possible ploys. Moreover, the risk of detection has been minimal because of the complexity of bookkeeping on Pentagon contracts and because one supplier may be simultaneously working on several contracts, making it possible to juggle charges between them. Not only have audits been intermittent, but only in 1982 did the Department of Defense establish a highly professional investigative agency, the Defense Criminal Investigative Service (DCIS).

Two egregious examples of procurement fraud in recent years, involving Litton Industries and the Sundstrand Corporation, typify both the motives and the technical ingenuity often involved. Both frauds share another distinction—the size of the penalties imposed, which in each case set a record. Litton Industries, a large conglomerate with headquarters in Beverly Hills, California, suffered less embarrassment than did Sundstrand, for its 1986 scandal was confined to a division of a subsidiary—Clifton Precision, Special Devices Division, a unit of Litton Systems, Inc., the parent company's giant defense subsidiary. Clifton Precision's Special Devices was a small outfit, then located in Drexel Hill, Pennsylvania, employing about four hundred people and doing a volume of business of around $25 million a year; it produced aircraft instruments and radar equipment. So specialized were its products that the Defense Department used it as a sole-source supplier, which meant of course that it had no competitors to bid against. It worked on the basis of fixed-price contracts—costs plus a percentage for profit, generally 15 to 20 percent. When a new contract was in the offing, Clifton would prepare a pricing proposal that set forth all its costs, including the cost of materials to be purchased from outside sources. The Defense Department often conducted a "preaward audit" to examine these figures, after which negotiations would ensue to establish the contract price. On some jobs Clifton Precision was a prime contractor; on others it served as a subcontractor for other Pentagon prime contractors, but the price-fixing procedure—and the frauds—were the same in both instances.

From 1975 through 1984, the government was later to charge, Clifton Precision developed enormous skill in inflating its stipulated costs and thus increasing its profit margins on Pentagon business. Indeed, the indictment in the case reads like an instruction book in how to undermine the system. Prior to negotiations, for example, Clifton employees would obtain price quotations from component suppliers from whom the company had no intention of buying, for the same items could be obtained more cheaply elsewhere. Alternatively, Clifton would go to regular suppliers and request inflated prices. An even simpler ploy, when the business relationship was cozy enough, was to obtain blank quotation forms from suppliers; the Clifton purchasing office would then fill them in. Employees even kept separate typewriter wheels in a drawer for each cooperating supplier, so that the quotation sheets did not all bear the same typeface. On other occasions, the accounting office would quote real prices taken from suppliers' catalogs, neglecting to mention the volume discount that it would obtain for buying in bulk. Sometimes the company received rebates, which it neglected to pass on to the government. Around the office, the price inflation was commonly referred to as "chicken fat."

Responsible for the scheme in the first instance was Roland Edward Fisher, vice president and general manager of Clifton's Special Devices Division. He would set the price he wanted on each contract, delegating the execution of the fraud to Michael J. Millspaugh, who at different times carried the titles of manager of cost accounting, controller, and director of the office of administration and finance. Millspaugh was responsible for preparing the contract proposals, and he selected the components whose prices were to be doctored. Millspaugh, in turn, delegated much of the actual work to Joseph DiLiberto, who served at different times as purchasing manager and materials manager. It was his job to gather the phony pricing data; among other things, he had the chore of forging suppliers' signatures on those blank quotation forms.

DiLiberto, a man in his sixties when the scheme started, was generally regarded as a capable purchasing agent, according to Robert I. Jacobs, the DCIS agent who helped develop the case. Jacobs maintains that DiLiberto went along with the scheme because he felt he had no alternative. He cooperated so as "not to make waves until he would retire. He knew he would never get another job. He never got anything out of it." His superior, Michael Millspaugh, was still in his twenties when the scam started. He was a talented man of obvious ambition who received successive promotions. His motive, again according to Jacobs, was "to be a good soldier and get ahead." Jacobs believes that Fisher, who controlled the operation, had an equally understandable goal: to improve the bottom line of his division and to advance his own career at Litton.

The government's first whiff of suspicion that something was amiss came in 1984, when a representative of the Defense Contract Audit Agency subjected one of Clifton's contracts to what is known as a "postaward audit." It is an occasional thing, done on a spot-check basis. Among other chores, the auditor compared the prices that the company had paid to suppliers with the price quotations that it had shown on its original contract proposal, which had been examined at a routine "preaward audit." A pattern soon emerged—the actual prices were often considerably lower than the projected prices. The contract price, of course, had been set on the basis of the earlier quotations—which suggested that the company had rigged its cost figures in order to boost profits. Clifton's representatives could not adequately explain the discrepancy.

Litton ultimately paid more than $100,000 in a civil settlement, but a criminal investigation was nonetheless launched. DiLiberto was induced to cooperate without much trouble; his assistance led to the unraveling of the scheme. In July 1986, the government obtained a 325-count indictment, alleging violations of the False Claims Act, mail fraud, and concealment of material facts; the document lists 45 contracts in which Litton was charged with defrauding the government of $6.3 million. DiLiberto implicated Millspaugh, who held out for a time but capitulated several days before his trial and agreed to cooperate with the government. As so often happens in these cases, once Millspaugh began to talk he, in turn, implicated his superior, Fisher, in the chain of guilt. He stated that not only did Fisher tell him the price he wanted for each contract, but that Fisher directed his accounting department to keep track of its true cost until it was finished.

Litton Systems, Inc., as well as DiLiberto and Millspaugh, pled guilty. Fisher was convicted in a trial in which Millspaugh, among others, testified against him. He subsequently lost an appeal. Litton had to pay $15 million in fines, restitution, damages and interest. DiLiberto got off with probation and a $10,000 fine; Millspaugh received a year in jail and a $10,000 fine, but Fisher got three years, plus a $5,000 fine.[17]

Litton Systems' $15 million payment held the record as the largest procurement fraud penalty for two years. In March 1988, in a settlement that did not involve any admission of wrongdoing, Bell Helicopter, a unit of Textron, Inc., agreed to pay the government $69 million in cash for overcharges on aircraft parts; it also agreed to furnish several million dollars worth of new parts.[18] Then, in October 1988, came a blockbuster settlement that easily captured the record for criminal or civil cases— an agreement by the Sundstrand Corporation to plead guilty to four counts of a criminal information and pay $115 million in "restitution, damages, penalties, fines and costs," as the plea agreement put it.[19] At the same time, a subsidiary called Sundstrand Data Control of Redmond, Washington, settled a federal overbilling case by agreeing to a guilty plea to one count and a payment of $12.3 million.[20]

Sundstrand, a manufacturer of aerospace equipment and other industrial parts with an annual sales volume in excess of $1 billion, had long been a major defense contractor, selling the Pentagon $574 million worth of merchandise in 1987, considerably more than its sales to the civilian aerospace industry. Its $115 million penalty was actually for four separate but concurrent crimes, the largest of which illustrates how fierce competitive pressures—in the absence of ethical constraints—make fraud an easy alternative to assuming the risk of failure.

Unlike the Clifton Precision unit of Litton Industries, the Sundstrand Corporation had to bid competitively for major contracts. Competitive bidding is clearly the best method of avoiding favoritism and achieving the cheapest deal for the buyer—so long as it is not circumvented. Sundstrand subverted the system by purposely underbidding to get contracts and then disguising its cost overruns in such a fashion that the Pentagon ended up paying for them. Such were the charges in one key count in the four to which Sundstrand pled guilty. Prosecutors alleged that from at least August 12, 1981, to at least June 3, 1985, Sundstrand defrauded the government of "millions of dollars"—no exact sum is specified—in concealed cost overruns on design and development contracts.

The conspiracy worked in this way, as the government explained in a memorandum filed in court: After Sundstrand's Advanced Technology Group received a request to bid on a design and development contract for a new piece of equipment, the engineers would calculate the number of hours needed to complete the work. From this data Sundstrand's pricing department would then determine the cost in dollars, add on a profit figure, and come up with a bid proposal. But then, according to the government's memo, "prior to the submission of Sundstrand's bid . . . or during the negotiation stage . . . Sundstrand would reduce its bid to a figure which was no longer sufficient to insure that Sundstrand would recover all of its costs under the contract."[21] On occasion, Sundstrand accidentally underbid by miscalculating its costs.

In either case, once the company got the contract, it recouped its position in the same way. For each contract, it set up a Total Manufacturing Cost budget that equaled the contractual price. Costs were regularly charged to the TMC until it was exhausted, at which point the company wrote a memo saying that work had been completed and the account was closed. Thereafter the ongoing costs of the contract were charged to one or another overhead account. How this was accomplished was technically complicated but is worth describing to illustrate the intricacy of these schemes. Sundstrand was regularly paid sums for overhead expenses that represented a percentage of the contract price. The overhead accounts, consisting of many items, were maintained to allow a periodic check by auditors of the accuracy of the percentages used. By inflating the overhead accounts with cost overruns, Sundstrand effectively inflated its overhead percentages and thereby recouped the money that it had lost by underbidding.

To foil the DOD auditors, who were located on Sundstrand's premises due to the volume of its defense work, the company engaged in an elaborate cover-up, falsely describing the accounting practices that it was using and even denying the auditors access to engineers whom they wished to question. But it was the persistence of resident auditor Michael S. McConnell that broke the cost overrun scam and made the criminal case possible. McConnell later told the *New York Times* that he had been given the runaround by the higher-ups, but that middle-management executives were willing to cooperate.[22]

While all this was going on, Sundstrand was enriching itself at the expense of the government through a huge tax scam. Starting in 1979, Sundstrand periodically shipped excess aircraft parts to a warehouse thirty miles away owned by the Sajac Company, which specialized in warehousing goods. Ostensibly Sundstrand sold the goods to Sajac at prices that generated tax losses. But the sales were pursuant to a written agreement that effectively barred Sajac from selling the aircraft parts to any company but Sundstrand, for if it did so it first had to remove the

Sundstrand name and insignia—which made the equipment unusable under the regulations of the Federal Aviation Administration. At the same time, the agreement contained a formula to set the prices at which Sundstrand could buy back the parts as it needed them. Sajac also provided Sundstrand with a monthly computer tape, updating information on the parts it had on hand; the tape became part of Sundstrand's inventory control system.

This lucrative arrangement, which saved Sundstrand millions in taxes—again the government did not provide a precise figure—remained undisturbed until April 1983 when the IRS issued Revenue Ruling 83-59 knocking down a tax-saving scheme much the same as Sundstrand's: the IRS argued that no true sale occurred because the "seller" retained too much control over the items presumably sold. The ruling gave pause to Sundstrand executives but did not prompt them to end the scheme. Instead, Sundstrand wrote a new contract with Sajac to disguise its continuing control over the parts and thereby hoodwink the IRS. The old buy-back formula was deleted and replaced by an oral agreement. The tax losses continued.

Nor was this all. The habit of corporate theft, once it starts, apparently embraces petty as well as grand larceny. Another criminal count to which Sundstrand pled guilty involved a multiplicity of personal expense items that Sundstrand executives fobbed off on the Pentagon. The variety of expenses dumped into the general and administrative (G&A) account, for which the Pentagon paid, made for hilarious reading when the case broke—nonbusiness travel and travel by executives' spouses, clothing, saunas, golf, country club dues, movies, jewelry, airline club memberships, dog kennels, snowplowing at executives' homes, radar detectors. Sundstrand accountants also included various expenses of the company's Data Control unit in Washington State in the G&A account of the aviation unit in Rockford, Illinois. This had the happy consequence of (fraudulently) inflating the corporation's total reimbursement by $800,000 a year, according to one internal Sundstrand memorandum.

Sundstrand's largess—again at government expense—was also extended to various Pentagon employees involved in contract negotiations and supervision. It had long been against Defense Department regulations for its employees to receive anything of value from a contractor, no matter how trifling, but this did not deter Sundstrand executives from proffering the normal small change of business entertainment—lunches, dinners, tickets to theater and sporting events, and the odd bottle of spirits. No bribery was alleged: over a seven-year period, these trifles came to a mere $100,000. Inasmuch as these favors were illegal to the recipient, a scheme was devised so that executives who extended hospitality did not have to note on their expense accounts the name and business affiliation of the recipient but could merely report "government official." When that tag was regarded as too compromising, the term "customer" was allowed to suffice. It proved to be an ineffective cover-up by the time the auditors got through with Sundstrand.

The $115 million penalty was not the only sanction that Sundstrand suffered. For several months, the Pentagon suspended its right to bid on new contracts. Three months after its guilty plea, Sundstrand announced that it had disciplined several employees. Five were fired or allowed to resign. Eight were reprimanded by letter, with four of them also receiving pay cuts and two pay freezes. The penalty for four others was only "special training."[23] In addition, Evans W. Erickson, chairman and chief executive officer, retired at the end of 1988 after eight years in the post. He stated that the windup of the criminal aspects of the case made it an appropriate moment for him to "pursue personal interests."[24] And as pledged in its plea agreement, Sundstrand instituted what the document quaintly called an "integrity assurance program" as a guarantee of future good behavior.

Procurement fraud has taken other forms as well. Strenuous competition to win defense contracts has put a premium on obtaining inside information about Pentagon acquisition plans, not to speak of intervening in the procurement process in ways that might charitably be called informal. These services have typically been provided by a small band of Washington consultants who are generally paid by monthly retainer. By no means are all defense consultants crooked—most may indeed be honest—and there are certainly legitimate services that a consultant can provide, guiding would-be contractors through the Pentagon's bewildering and often shifting procedures and advising them how to structure their submissions. Typically, consultants have vast expertise, gained through years of service in the very DOD agencies that they are now lobbying. The consultant may well be worth $2,000 to $5,000 a month for legitimate advice and introductions alone—and far more if willing to exploit contacts in ways that cross the line of legality or propriety.

The devious world of defense consultants was suddenly illuminated when a wide-ranging Justice Department investigation called Operation Ill Wind became public in mid-June 1988. The investigation had started two years before. According to Henry E. Hudson, then U.S. attorney for the Eastern District of Virginia,[25] it all began when a bidder on a Pentagon contract informed the FBI and the Naval Investigative Service (NIS) that a consultant had offered to sell him "proprietary type information" about the contract that belonged to a rival bidder. "The impression this bidder had was that this consultant could guarantee an award of the contract to him for a certain price," says Hudson. The informant agreed to cooperate with the FBI, which had him arrange another meeting with the consultant, who confirmed that the contraband information was available. This time, the FBI recorded the conversation, which enabled it to confront the consultant and secure his cooperation. The leads he provided soon developed into Operation Ill Wind, which was jointly conducted by the FBI and the NIS, with coordination provided by Hudson's office under the direction of Joseph J. Aronica, the lead prosecutor. The targets were consultants, Pentagon officials and employees, and executives of companies seeking contracts.

Over the course of the year, a huge body of evidence was collected as a result of thirty-eight court-authorized wiretaps, six "microphone implants" (more commonly known as bugs), and finally forty search warrants executed in offices and homes in twelve states one day in mid-June.[26] Those searches and seizures catapulted the case onto the front pages. Day by day, new details were added about specific allegations of bribery and trafficking in confidential information, much of it gleaned from the affidavits filed in federal court by FBI agents seeking search warrants. The FBI had to make a showing of probable cause to get a warrant, a process that required it to specify names—among them some of the country's biggest defense contractors—as well as putative events. The names inevitably found their way into print. So did some vigorous congressional rhetoric. Senator John W. Warner of Virginia, a former secretary of the navy, told a news conference that "it appears at first glance to be the worst case of alleged blatant exchange of gifts for proprietary information."[27] Senator Charles Grassley of Iowa, another Republican and an inveterate critic of procurement practices, exclaimed, "What will be exposed here will be beyond anyone's wildest imagination."[28] News stories predicted a flock of indictments in the course of the summer. But by the end of 1988, no indictments had yet been returned by a grand jury sitting in Alexandria, Virginia, and stories began to appear suggesting that Operation Ill Wind had been hyped up. "Ill Wind a Scandal Overblown?" read a headline over a disenchanted story in the *Washington Post* of December 27, 1988.

The investigation may not have initially lived up to its first, breathless billing, but in the years that followed it produced impressive results. By June 1992, six corporations had been convicted, as well as fifty individuals. The highest-ranking Pentagon official to be convicted was Melvyn R. Paisley, a former assistant secretary of the navy for research, engineering and systems, whose guilty plea to three counts involving conspiracy, bribery, and defrauding the United States led to a four-year sentence and a $50,000 fine. In one instance, Paisley had shared in a large payoff for helping an Israeli company obtain a contract for a pilotless reconnaissance aircraft. In another, for valued though illegal assistance to the Sperry Corporation (Sperry merged with Burroughs to become Unisys in 1986), the bribe was disguised in the form of a greatly inflated payment for a condominium owned by Paisley.[29]

Two months after Paisley's plea, the prosecutors convicted another prize target, Victor D. Cohen, a top procurement official in the office of the assistant secretary of the air force, who also pled guilty to charges of bribery and conspiracy to defraud the government. Cohen received a thirty-three-month sentence. Of the forty-eight other individuals convicted, two received sentences of thirty-two months and three, twenty-seven months.[30]

The distinction of being the biggest corporate offender in the area of procurement fraud, as ranked by the size of the negotiated penalty, was bestowed on Sperry/Unisys (the term for the company used in the court documents). In September 1991, the corporation pled guilty to eight criminal counts involving conspiracy to defraud the United States, bribery of a public official, and the filing of false claims, among other offenses, and agreed to pay $190 million—a sum that far exceeded Sundstrand's burden. Five million dollars went for criminal fines, $162 million for civil damages and penalties, $5 million for reimbursement of the government's investigative cost, and another $18 million for the Justice Department's Asset Forfeiture Fund, to be spent, in a nice stroke of poetic justice, on law enforcement.[31]

The penalties imposed on other erring corporations, which in each case also included the cost of the investigations, were more modest, though hardly slaps on the wrist. The Loral Corporation paid the next-largest sum—$5,770,000—after pleading guilty to three counts. In addition, Loral agreed in its plea bargain to modify its air force contract for an "advanced radar warning receiver" so that the company would assume a larger share of expected cost overruns, thereby eliminating all possibility of profit and saving the government between $4.5 million and $6.5 million.[32]

Teledyne Industries, Inc., the Hazeltine Corporation (a subsidiary of Emerson Electric), Whittaker Command and Control Systems, and Cubic Defense Systems, Inc., all pled guilty to the same offenses, as well as some others. Teledyne, as mentioned earlier in the chapter, sustained fines and penalties exceeding $4 million. Cubic had to disgorge a bit more—$4.65 million. Whittaker paid $3.5 million and Hazeltine $1.91 million.[33]

The court documents in the various cases outline a variety of sleazy scenarios in which corporate executives hired Washington consultants with good Pentagon contacts. For a price, these Pentagon stalwarts were in a position to reveal confidential plans as well as tips on what rival bidders were proposing, and they could sometimes persuade contracting authorities to alter specifications and otherwise tailor the deal to benefit the client company.

In one of the more blatant cases, the Hazeltine Corporation in 1986 hired an Alexandria, Virginia, consultant named William L. Parkin to help get a production contract for radar test sets, for which it had previously completed a research and development contract. Parkin's compensation was a modest $2,000 a month (later raised to $5,000), but there was also an option in the contract that allowed Hazeltine to engage him further, for a fee of either $30,000 or $50,000, to prepare surveys of the potential U.S. or worldwide markets for the company's products. Through intercepted conversations, however, the government learned that the additional payments were actually to reward Parkin if Hazeltine succeeded in winning the contract, which the government estimated to be worth about $150 million. Hazeltine had a powerful competitor in a company called Gould, which had also completed a prior research and development contract for the devices.

The key Defense Department figure in the scheme was Stuart E. Berlin, who bore the elaborate title of supervisory electronics engineer and branch head of ship systems engineering at the Naval Air Systems Command in Virginia. He was privy to a lot of information about the contract and was a member of the procurement review board that was to decide the competition. Parkin, however, did not deal directly with Berlin but with another consultant named Fred H. Lackner, based in California, who relayed requests to Berlin while Parkin dealt directly with Hazeltine officials. Parkin, Lackner, and Berlin agreed to share all the proceeds from Hazeltine, but the two consultants shortchanged Berlin and paid him a mere $2,500.

For that paltry sum, Berlin provided Hazeltine with a "for official use only" draft of the navy acquisition plan for the devices, as well as estimates of the minimum and maximum amounts of the test sets likely to be purchased each year and various government budget figures—useful information to anyone planning to bid. Later on, while the government was still preparing its acquisition program, Parkin asked Hazeltine executives "for their input about what they wanted the Navy to emphasize in the evaluation criteria." In the end, some of Hazeltine's suggestions were adopted.

Bidding for the contract began early in 1988. It was a two-stage process, a typical DOD procedure. Each bidder makes an initial offer. After evaluating the bids, DOD asks each company still in the running for what is known as a BAFO—its best and final offer. In light of this procedure, Parkin suggested a clever strategy to Hazeltine: bid high initially; Parkin would then leak Hazeltine's bid to Gould, making it likely that Gould would not lower its BAFO as much as it might otherwise have done. Hazeltine would then have an excellent chance of submitting a final offer below Gould's. As the weeks passed, the scheme seemed to be working well. Parkin funneled to the company confidential information as to what the navy expected the line-by-line contract cost to be and its overall target price. Hazeltine then bid a little more than $200 million, far more than it knew the navy wanted. Gould came in about $50 million lower; Hazeltine was apprised of this. But before Hazeltine could undercut Gould and complete the final round of bidding, the Ill Wind investigation became public and the game ended. When the FBI and the NIS conducted their searches, they were able to find documentary corroboration of the information that had been illegally passed to Hazeltine.

In all, Hazeltine's several payments to Parkin totalled $38,000. Parkin in turn remitted $14,500 to Lackner, who paid Berlin his meager $2,500.[34]

All three pled guilty to bribery and other charges; Parkin and Berlin received sentences of twenty-six months, Lackner twenty-seven months. Joseph R. Colarusso, an executive vice president of Hazeltine with whom Parkin dealt, got a ten-month sentence and a $30,000 fine, and Charles A. Furciniti, a Hazeltine marketing vice president, pulled three months and a $20,000 fine.[35]

While Ill Wind was moving through the courts, a parallel and unrelated investigation in Hudson's office—this one called Operation Uncover—led to the plea bargains of Boeing, Grumman, Hughes Aircraft, RCA, and Raytheon.[36] The charges did not involve bribery or the leaking of information on rival bids or the tailoring of specifications to a contractor's needs, but rather the illegal possession and dissemination of classified Pentagon planning and budget documents. Despite security clearances held by many employees, none of the companies were authorized to possess copies of such basic Pentagon papers as the DOD's "PPBs" (its overall plan, program, and budget) or each military service's "POM" (its program objective memorandum), which outlined the army's or the navy's or the air force's priority list of weapons systems, or the "PDMs" (the program decision memorandums of the Defense Resources Board, produced after the board had scrutinized the various POMs).

This alphabet soup of planning and budgetary documents was naturally of great value to large defense contractors, giving them a competitive edge. But trafficking in forbidden paper had long been illegal. Nevertheless, for a period of several years in the late 1970s and 1980s, there was a brisk underground exchange of classified Pentagon documents among employees of different companies. How the documents had been initially obtained was never publicly made clear, but there was ample evidence of hoards of illegal paper on the premises of various companies. Some lower-level employees went to prison, and the corporations paid fines and civil penalties ranging from $2.5 million in the case of Grumman to $5.2 million for Boeing. Were it not for the embarrassing publicity, the companies might well have figured it was worth a few million for a lengthy, unimpeded peek into the back rooms of the Pentagon.[37]

From the sampling of cases in this chapter and the previous one it is clear that corporate fraud covers a broad spectrum—from the kind of artless, irresponsible deception of the Chrysler odometer case to the complexly designed schemes to inflate the bottom line in the Litton and

Sundstrand cases. The check overdrafting fraud that E. F. Hutton perpetrated falls somewhere in between.

Although it is clear that the Hutton scam was fraudulent, it is conceivable that at least some of those involved might not have seen anything wrong in getting a free ride from some somnolent provincial banks. Anyone presiding over the operation, however, would have been preposterously naive not to have been aware of wrongdoing. On the other hand, the fraudulent intent of the Hertz, Beech-Nut, Litton, and Sundstrand schemes was as clear-cut as a bank robbery. So was the motive: to improve performance at whatever cost. Beech-Nut was in a highly competitive situation, as one of three major baby-food producers. The auto rental industry is a competitive jungle, which may explain why the top managers of Hertz did not examine what was going on in their accident control precincts. Sundstrand's Advanced Technology Group let nothing stand in its way in striving to get contracts. Executives had the excuse of sheer necessity—not that the excuse was ever publicly voiced—in underbidding on contracts. They were not trying to increase the yield of their contracts, but simply to get the work. No such excuse can be made for Litton's Clifton Precision fraud, for the division was guaranteed the job as sole-source supplier. The general manager was simply after increased profits. For any division manager, success rides with the fortunes of his operation. That is often the mainspring of fraud.

Litton's Clifton Precision scam, like so many others, went undetected for years. Only a serendipitous discovery by an auditor sounded the alarm. While there are a plethora of fraud cases, particularly in defense industry, only a relatively small number are discovered and result in prosecution (though the record has improved in recent years). As previously suggested, ambitious and shortsighted managers in defense industries can still play a version of audit roulette, gambling that the scrutiny of the Defense Contract Audit Agency will not land on them or that their labyrinthine deceptions will be impenetrable. If they do a cost-benefit analysis, they may well decide that the risk is tenuous but the gain certain.

How that perception might be reversed is the subject, among other things, of the final chapter.

CHAPTER 9

WHAT TO DO?

Corporate crime might paradoxically be characterized as both aberrant and normal; it is difficult to repress because its sources are so deep-rooted. It is by definition deviant behavior because it violates the law; it also violates the canons of ethics to which almost everybody subscribes formally. Yet, in many situations, illegal activity is a natural reaction to the conflicts and pressures that afflict much of business. The crimes that we have been dealing with are usually not impulsive or mere expressions of irresponsibility; they represent not aberrations so much as alternative ways of doing business. In many circumstances, illegal methods are as authentic an expression of business mores as legal ones.

Illustrations abound. In small retail business, skimming cash is a widely practiced tax dodge, as the IRS tax gap figures prove; an amoralist would view it as a way of cutting costs. To many salesmen in highly competitive fields, kickbacks to purchasing agents are a normal response to the pressures of combat. The same can be said of the procurement frauds that victimize the Pentagon, as was argued in the last chapter.

Respectable and otherwise ethical citizens readily commit business crimes in large part because they do not perceive such offenses to be truly criminal. Relevant here is the frequently drawn distinction between malum in se—a crime in itself, violative of natural law and forbidden in every civilized society—and malum prohibitum, a purely statutory offense that represents legislative taste and may vary from country to country even in the same era. As a well-known defense lawyer once explained to me, "We all grew up in an environment in which we learned that thou shalt not murder, rape, rob, probably not pay off a public official—but not that it was a crime to fix prices. These business crimes are perceived by individual actors as victimless." Fears of detection might deter price-fixing, but hardly pangs of conscience.

To lawbreakers, the notion of victim seems to be an especially arbitrary, intellectual construct in the case of price-fixing, insider trading, and tax cheating. Indeed, insider traders frequently argue that no one is hurt by their activity, for they will not concede that an unfair profit captured by one person is of necessity denied to someone else not privy to the inside information. Price-fixing obviously harms the customer, not to speak of the economy in general, but the harm seems marginal to those involved in the practice and is certainly not life threatening. On the other hand, price fixers maintain that they are saving the jobs of their employees by safeguarding their company from ruinous competition. As for cheating the tax collector, only prosecutors and judges seem to regard the IRS as a proxy for the nation and its citizens; there may be no vaguer victim than the largest conceivable collectivity. Moreover, in an era when so many politicians have campaigned successfully against Washington, big governmnent is widely regarded as the enemy—and what agency better personifies it than the IRS?

While corporate crime is widespread, it does not infest every sector of business. It flourishes only where conditions are appropriate, generally when both the pressures on managerial performance and the opportunity to cheat are present in sufficient measure. Sometimes pressure is less important than opportunity. Retail businesses move mountains of cash, but, as noted in the chapter on tax evasion, large stores are constrained from skimming by the financial controls set in place to thwart embezzling. Small establishments have no such inhibitions and often cannot resist the abundant opportunities to squirrel away cash.

Competitive stress has little to do with the impulse to trade on inside information. The practice flourished when Wall Street was awash in profits; opportunity was all that was required. On the other hand, declining business and incessant price cutting often encourage conspiracies to fix prices. Not in all industries, of course. Certain structural conditions are required: relatively undifferentiated products, a small enough group of competitors to be corralled into a price agreement—and often a history of past conspiracies.

Behavior that is so deep-seated, financially beneficial, easily rationalized, and sanctioned by custom is obviously difficult to change. But corporate crime must be repressed—like all crime it cannot be eradicated—lest it grow even more rampant. The country cannot afford cynical indifference or a bemused tolerance toward business corruption because its costs, as previously argued, are far too high—to the consumer, to economic efficiency, to the nation's treasury, above all to the moral tone of the community.

The job of repressing business crime devolves on corporate America as well as on government. At first glance, this may seem paradoxical, for corporate gain motivates all of the crimes we have been analyzing. But business crime, to put it mildly, is hardly an unmixed blessing, especially to large corporations. Antitrust violations and defense procurement fraud inflate the bottom line, to be sure; they can be exceedingly beneficial to the company—unless and until they are detected. Then crisis breaks, with huge fines, compulsory restitution, multiple damages, and even mandatory reimbursement of the cost of the investigation, not to speak of jail terms for the ringleaders and public ignominy for the entire corporation. Top executives are not being insincere when they express their determination to clean up.

Before examining what measures business can employ, we take up government's role first. While larger and more imaginative enforcement efforts are required, it must be conceded that the situation has improved somewhat in recent years. There was a time, a dozen or more years ago, when a cynic could reasonably scoff that an errant corporate executive received so lenient a sentence—generally a fine and probation—that it constituted more of a license fee than a penalty. No longer. Both prison terms and fines have been substantially increased in several key areas, as previously noted. Until 1974, price-fixing was a misdemeanor, with imprisonment limited to twelve months. That year Congress made the offense a felony, providing for prison sentences of up to three years and corporate fines as high as $1 million—since raised to $10 million. In 1988, criminal penalties for insider trading were significantly strengthened, with the maximum sentence going from five to ten years and fines rising tenfold to $1 million. The SEC is also empowered to exact triple damages for any illegal monetary gain realized. More severe sanctions against kickbacks among government contractors and subcontractors were also legislated in 1986. The maximum prison term rose from two to ten years and fines, previously limited to $10,000, were increased to $250,000 in the case of individuals and $1 million for corporations.

The usefulness of imprisonment as a deterrent for corporate offenders, as contrasted with other criminals, cannot be overstressed. It is a
commonplace in criminology that traditional criminals—burglars,
muggers, hijackers, loan sharks, extortionists, drug dealers, and racketeers of all sorts—are not significantly deterred by the threat of being
locked up. Many are likely to have served time, often as early as their
juvenile years, so the prospect neither alarms them nor threatens social
obloquy in their set. Getting jailed is just one of the hazards of their trade,
whose pain can often be mitigated through plea bargaining.

The attitudes of middle-class corporate executives are quite different.
They have never been inured to a periodic loss of freedom. Almost all
of them, judging by their later comments, never thought they would be
caught. Many of them illogically claim that they were aware that their
activities were illegal but did not regard them as criminal. When caught,
they are shocked at the prospect of a prison term and even more shocked
by the reality of it. Thus, the conventional wisdom is that potential corporate offenders can be deterred by the threat of incarceration, so long
as the threat is made credible by rigorous law enforcement. The theory would seem to have been validated by the singularly low level of recidivism among corporate criminals who have been caught.

Judges certainly believe in the deterrent effect of prison sentences,
which have become notably stiffer in recent years. In 1960, the business
community was shocked when executives of General Electric, Westinghouse,
and other top companies who had participated in price-fixing rings
were sentenced to thirty days in prison, plus modest fines. The offense
had rarely brought jail terms before. Recently, however, six- and nine-
month sentences have become common. For other forms of corporate
crime, such as procurement fraud and tax evasion, multiyear penalties
are not uncommon. In sentencing statements, judges frequently stress
the exemplary character of the penalties, as well as the unfairness of a
modest sentence for a white-collar offender while a blue-collar criminal, who usually makes off with much less money, is hit with the book.

The trend toward heavier sentences will continue, if only because of
the U.S. Sentencing Commission. The commission, an independent agency in the judicial branch, was established as a result of the Comprehensive
Crime Control Act of 1984 with the task of promulgating sentencing
guidelines for federal courts that would eliminate the wide disparities in
the penalties imposed for the same offenses. After lengthy deliberations,

the commission published a thick set of guidelines taking effect on November 1, 1987, which means for crimes committed after that date.[1] The guidelines all relate to a numerical table, which determines length of imprisonment according to the degree of seriousness of the crime involved. Mitigating factors in the commission of an offense lower the level of penalty; magnifying factors raise it. A judge who wants to deviate from the guidelines must explain the exceptional circumstances prompting that action. The new system also abolishes parole; a term of imprisonment can only be reduced by time off for good behavior.

The effect of the guidelines will be to increase penalties for business crime—that is, to raise the average penalty by raising the lowest. The Sentencing Commission was quite clear in its intent. In its guidelines for antitrust violations, the commission increased the prison term by one level if the offense involved bid rigging. It then geared the penalty to the "volume of commerce attributable to the defendant"—subtracting one level if it involved less than $1 million, making no adjustment for a volume of between $1 million and $4 million, and thereafter raising the level step by step. If the defendant's actions affected over $50 million in economic activity, the penalty would go up by three levels. Fines are also determined by the dollar volume influenced; for an individual it ranges between 4 and 10 percent of the sum affected, but no less than $20,000, and for a corporation, 20 to 50 percent, with a minimum fine of $100,000. For a small company, that makes dabbling in price-fixing a very serious business.

The net effect of all this in price-fixing cases, says the commission, is "that prison terms should become much more common, and usually longer, than is currently typical." The guidelines translate into imprisonment of at least four months in the great majority of cases prosecuted, with the courts having the discretion to impose much longer terms. By contrast, when the guidelines were published, only 39 percent of convicted defendants received prison terms, with the average period forty-five days. The commission commented: "Tying the offense level to the scale or scope of the offense is important in order to ensure that the sanction is in fact punitive and that there is an incentive to desist from a violation once it has begun."[2] In similar fashion, the guidelines also increase average prison terms for tax evasion.[3]

Not enough time has gone by to assess the full impact of the guidelines, but they have had some influence on crimes committed even before

November 1987, for prosecutors frequently allude to the guidelines in recommending sentences for these earlier crimes and judges can heed the argument if they wish. In 1991, the commission supplemented its original guidelines with a new set of corporate penalties. In 1987 the commission only dealt with corporate fines for antitrust violations. Now it produced elaborate criteria for many different crimes, depending on severity, how high knowledge of the crime went in the corporation, and whether the company sought to thwart government investigators or cooperated with them. Fines could soar into the many millions. It is too soon, of course, to know the deterrent effect of these mandatory penalties.

Both the statutory penalties and the sentencing guidelines are adequate. The real problem is the nature of the enforcement effort. The main burden falls on the federal government, though in recent years state attorneys general have become increasingly active, particularly in the field of consumer fraud, and various state tax departments have shown an encouraging interest in better enforcement of their own tax laws. To give credit where it is due, the federal enforcement effort has also been stepped up since the mid-1980s—in the fields of criminal antitrust violations, insider trading and other security frauds, defense procurement fraud, and defense-related kickbacks. By contrast, enforcement of the federal tax laws has fallen off, as the declining audit ratios show.

If one takes a longer view, it is apparent that enforcement tends to be cyclical and even faddish. Thus, in the 1980s the SEC began its well-publicized drive against insider trading. Why then? The offense particularly interested the new chairman of the SEC. But the commission had first made a big fuss about insider trading in the Texas Gulf Sulphur case in 1965 and thereafter showed only intermittent interest in the field; the first criminal conviction did not occur until 1977 (and was later reversed by the Supreme Court). Yet there was every reason to believe that insider trading went on continuously throughout the period; it was, after all, one of the oldest phenomena of the stock market. But for many years in the 1970s the SEC was preoccupied with the nondisclosure by American companies of foreign bribery, a new area into which it plunged after an investigation by a committee headed by Senator Frank Church.

The antitrust division of the Justice Department pressed its celebrated case against the electrical equipment manufacturers in 1959 and 1960. Thereafter, the division did not make another big splash in the criminal field until the 1970s, when it produced a successful run of cases in the forest-products industries—cardboard and corrugated boxes, fine paper, and so on. In the 1980s, it got deeply involved in the electrical construction field and road building—through happy accident, as previously related. The division went after targets of opportunity wherever they popped up.

With these crimes the increase in enforcement activity started from a relatively low base (which makes it no less welcome). At first glance, it may seem curious that more vigorous enforcement began under an avowedly probusiness administration. To be sure, the Reagan administration was for some years anything but vigorous about environmental offenses; however in the areas we have explored the administration's prosecutors could not be faulted for lack of energy. How to account for the paradox?

To start with, the assumption that an ideological predisposition in favor of business will tend to excuse all business delinquencies is invalid. The very fact that the administration favored widespread deregulation, for which it was frequently criticized, may have made it more eager to prove its good faith by attacking the kinds of business behavior that no ideology could defend. The Justice Department's antitrust division in the Reagan years was often criticized by liberals for being too tolerant of the massive merger movement. The critical barrage may well have inspired each head of the division to seek to validate his trust-busting credentials by mounting vigorous efforts against price-fixing and bid rigging.

Another consideration that should never be overlooked is the professional pride and dedication (not too strong a word) of the staff lawyers in a place like the antitrust division. They are in the business of making cases in a highly technical area of the law, and they are zealous in pursuit of violators, whatever the ideological coloration of the administration in office. Each of them also has a personal stake in success: a prosecutor's achievement is measured by the number of convictions. The same point can be made, of course, about U.S. attorneys' offices around the country, and it is notable that in the probusiness Reagan years the federal prosecutors in Manhattan, Chicago and Los Angeles made some of their most publicized cases in the area of business crime—the insider-trading cases in New York, the Sundstrand case in Chicago, and the defense industry kickback cases in Los Angeles. In all these operations, there is an autonomous institutional dynamic at work that cannot be discounted.

Some business critics maintain that the problem is not insufficient law enforcement but excessive prosecutorial zeal. A major target for attack has been the government's use of the Racketeer Influenced and Corrupt Organizations (RICO) statute in a few indictments for business crime. The RICO law makes a supercrime with superpenalties out of a string of garden variety felonies. Under RICO, a defendant can be convicted of a "pattern of racketeering" if guilty of as few as two felonies under federal or state law within a period of ten years of each other.

The main purpose of the statute, enacted in 1970, was to give federal prosecutors a strong weapon against traditional racketeers—extortionists, drug dealers, loan sharks, labor racketeers, and other mobsters—who invested their criminal profits in legitimate businesses and used the additional proceeds to further extend their illegal activities. If a pattern of racketeering could be proved—although only two substantive acts were required, more were usually spelled out in the indictment—the convicted defendant was subject not only to imprisonment but to the forfeiture of the assets derived from the "racketeering enterprise" and of his share of the enterprise itself. In many successful prosecutions, this meant not only businesses bought with ill-gotten gains but home, boat, automobiles. Moreover, the act provided for temporary surrender of assets before trial, if the prosecutors could persuade a judge, as they often did, that the assets might be dissipated before the legal proceedings were over. Such provisional forfeiture was by no means automatic; in 50 percent of the cases, prosecutors did not ask for it, and judges, if they agreed with the need, could also allow the defendant to post a bond to cover the value of the assets involved.

The attack on the use of RICO in white-collar cases has been advanced on two grounds: that Congress only meant it to apply to the traditional rackets and that the provisions for forfeiture give prosecutors an unfair weapon to coerce a guilty plea to lesser charges. There is no doubt that Congress's main targets were traditional mobsters, but there was enough discussion of the wider applicability of RICO while Congress was deliberating to suggest that its recent use against business defendants does not distort congressional intent. It would seem a reasonable use of the statute if the target of a prosecution was an ostensibly legitimate business much of whose activity was actually criminal; the existence of merely two or three "predicate" acts of wrongdoing within the time frame would hardly seem to be enough. The Justice Department has to approve all RICO prosecutions and has issued guidelines for its use, which may not always have been followed.

The forfeiture provisions of the law have received a good deal of unfavorable press attention, particularly in the *Wall Street Journal*, after the demise of Princeton-Newport, a small New Jersey securities firm that collapsed after some indicted partners forfeited assets and the others pulled out their funds. When convicted, the defendants were fined much less than the value of the sequestered assets. Then, when Drexel Burnham Lambert plea-bargained in 1989, admitting guilt to several counts, critics charged that the threat of forfeiture through a RICO conviction gave the prosecutors an enormously unfair advantage. The argument is not persuasive: the company could have avoided any pretrial freezing of assets by posting bond, and one has to presume the existence of an enormous racketeering enterprise if a conviction would have resulted in forfeiture of a magnitude that could collapse the firm. If the company was indeed that vulnerable, RICO would seem to have been used to good purpose. When Michael Milken pled guilty in April 1990, the threat of RICO was also invoked by his apologists as the reason he accepted a plea bargain. This is equally unpersuasive. It is hard to believe that a defendant with Milken's resources, if he felt himself to be innocent, would have admitted guilt to the serious charges to which he pled: conspiracy to defraud in order to enrich himself and Drexel, cheating customers, rigging the market, and helping a customer evade taxes, among other matters.

RICO is not the problem, nor is overzealous prosecution, though whatever the nature of the law there is always the possibility that a politically ambitious prosecutor will press too hard in a particular case. Rather than being oppressive, law enforcement is actually too weak, too intermittent, and too easily distracted by new targets of opportunity—all deficiencies that risk eroding the deterrent effect of stiffer sentences. Precisely because criminal behavior is so entrenched in certain industries, so bolstered by tradition and thus so plausibly excused, deterrence can only work when the police power of the state is perceived as an ever-looming presence.

The deterrent impact is obviously greatest while the SEC or the antitrust division or the IRS is making an aggressive drive in a particular industry or against a specific violation; a lot of larcenous schemes are likely to be aborted. At least that is the probability, for there is never much hard evidence, only informed impressions. Gary Lynch, the former SEC enforcement chief, believed that there was a decided falloff in insider trading on Wall Street after the agency's widely publicized spate of cases.[4] But what happens afterward? What if the SEC should neglect insider trading in favor of its other preoccupations? For a time, memories of what happened to Levine or Boesky or even Robert Freeman will remain vivid and inhibiting. But, after a time, memory fades and the sense of hazard recedes. In such circumstances, it is easy to predict that once again there will be an upsurge of insider trading.

The work of the antitrust division is even more discontinuous than that of the SEC. It is tipped to a particular violation in an industry. It makes a successful case. One case leads to another; before long the division seems to have cleaned up the industry. Then it moves on, rarely looking back, never making a return visit unless new information comes its way. It lacks the resources, through a network of contacts and informers, to undertake surveillance of industries that it has previously been preoccupied with. Unless there is a structural change in the industry, or a profound change in its mores, one can anticipate a return of bad habits.

The first requirement is to increase the funding and staffing of federal enforcement agencies. Many suffered from fiscal anemia owing to the budgetary constraints of the Reagan years, except for activities related to the much-touted war on drugs. Mention was previously made of the decrease in staff lawyers in the antitrust division in the 1980s. It is surely indisputable that 267 full-time lawyers in Washington and in seven regional offices across the country cannot adequately monitor the vast expanse of the American economy for violations of the Sherman Act, civil and criminal. The 43 percent decline in staff was entirely the result of a budget that in *nominal* dollars moved upward only slightly while the general price level was soaring. Thus, in fiscal 1980 the total budget authority was $43.5 million. It rose slightly to $44.8 million in 1981, thereafter declined gradually to $42.5 million in 1986, and then crept back to $45.3 million in 1990. For that year, the appropriation was actually cut by $15 million, with Congress mandating that the division make up the shortfall from fees charged (for the first time) to corporations filing applications for approval of proposed mergers. The fee for a so-called Hart-Scott-Rodino filing was set at a hefty $20,000. Congress anticipated that $20 million would be collected, but merger activity fell off during the year and only $13 million was realized. Ironically, the antitrust division is responsible for millions of dollars a year in fines paid by errant corporations, but it never sees that money, which disappears into the general accounts of the Treasury.[5]

The woefully inadequate number of IRS audits is largely attributable to budget limitations. The criminal investigation division (CI) of IRS has in recent years been burdened with responsibility for investigating money laundering and the tax offenses of drug traffickers, which limits the personnel it can devote to tax evasion by business and individuals. It is ludicrous that in all of the United States, in the fiscal year 1991, CI had only 201 undercover operations going on—and that included drug and money laundering cases as well as tax evasion.

Federal investigative efforts unrelated to the drug problem have suffered from short rations for some years. Top executives in the investigative agencies in the Bush administration (as in the Reagan administration) tend not to complain but to utter pieties about the need to prioritize, and the first priority has been the multi-billion-dollar war on drugs. That preoccupation, combined with the overhanging federal deficit, has scotched any impulse to propose dramatic expansion of enforcement efforts against business crime (except for a stepped-up campaign at the Justice Department against S&L fraud). Agency heads know that they will be slapped down by the Office of Management and Budget before their proposals can be presented to Congress. Increases in funding generally do little more than track inflation. Even the 1991 increase for enforcement activity received by the IRS was relatively modest, as was the one for 1992. And often the spending increases approved by the OMB have been further pared by the Congress. Enforcement will inevitably fall far short of its potential unless the money is made available.

Adequate funding is not all that is needed. Crime prevention as well as detection requires a more aggressive approach. Only the SEC, the IRS, and the Defense Department have adequate techniques to keep their jurisdictions under continual surveillance—the SEC by vetting stock prospectuses, proxy statements, annual reports, and so on as well as access to the market monitoring conducted by the stock exchanges and the National Association of Securities Dealers. The IRS and the Defense Department each have audit power, which if used broadly and frequently enough is a marvelous surveillance tool. The antitrust division and the fraud section of the criminal division at the Justice Department have no such facility. Nor do the U.S. attorney's offices around the country. There is no way to monitor the volume of kickbacks and bribery in the United States, among other things.

The antitrust division has tried at least one novel technique to turn up violations. In the 1970s, it experimented with computer programs tracking selling prices in various industries, trying to determine whether patterns emerged that suggested illegal activity. But not much could be determined from this analysis, and it was abandoned.

Writing in his 1978 book, *The Antitrust Paradox*, Robert H. Bork stated that "experience with antitrust suggests that there is far more price fixing in the economy than the enforcement authorities suggest. The major reason for the poor detection record is the paucity of Antitrust Division field offices. Field offices are located in a few major cities, and their staffs tend not to work at any distance from their bases." Bork proposed splitting up the Washington staff into several more offices,[6] presumably to establish roots in more communities so that the lawyers could get to know local business executives, learn how local industry operates, pick up helpful gossip, and detect more violations. (He did not actually specify what the lawyers would do in the field.) It is an intriguing idea, but the division now has one fewer office than when Bork wrote; once again the budget intervened. Currently, lawyers are often sent out from Washington headquarters to handle major cases. They usually spend all day in court and half the night working in their hotel rooms to bone up for the next day's session. As a consequence, they do not learn much more about the locals than they know from their cases. The current field offices handle some important cases and many more minor ones. But it is doubtful if sending one hundred more lawyers or so out from Washington would make much difference, assuming that many could be spared from headquarters duties. A lot more staff would have to be hired to set up a truly far-reaching field office network. A course in detective work would probably also be helpful.

The reward system should be expanded and better publicized. One point stressed earlier was about the serendipitous origins of so many major cases. A complaint from the Tennessee Valley Authority launched the electrical manufacturing cases of 1959–60. The Dennis Levine case began with an anonymous letter to the Merrill Lynch office in New York. The Gurary invoice-purchasing case was served up voluntarily to the U.S. attorney by a hard-pressed suspect in another case. The Hertz car-repair fraud came from an ex-employee with a grievance.

There is nothing wrong, of course, with an investigation starting from a tip; far from it. The case that walks in off the street is a commonplace of police work. It is a major function of police agencies, after all, to receive complaints from the public and referrals from other government agencies. Large monetary rewards are frequently offered in especially heinous or dramatic crimes—murders, kidnappings. Rewards are also offered in business crimes, but in this area an extraordinary degree of circumspection or embarrassment envelops the enforcement agencies.

It is almost as if it were infra dig to talk about money. No posters announcing rewards go up in post offices. The SEC does not placard the stock exchanges or brokerage offices with offers of lucre for information on insider trading. (And why is there none for tips involving market manipulation or fleecing a brokerage house customer or a host of other crimes over which the SEC has jurisdiction? Another law would be required, of course.) And, as previously noted, not a single reference to its reward program is to be found in any IRS publication.

One recommendation comes immediately to mind. The reward programs should be broadened. Why not also have rewards for revealing price-fixing and bid rigging? Why not provide an incentive for information on kickbacks? In companies where kickbacks flourish, many people may suspect them and some have hard knowledge. It would take a minimum of legislative draftmanship and relatively little money to establish a comprehensive reward system.

There are two main objections to such a proposal. One is that cash incentives may elicit a mountain of misinformation for every morsel of hard fact. The other is that encouraging citizens to be informers would create an insidious climate of betrayal and mistrust throughout society. The first hazard can be mitigated, and the second is vastly exaggerated. Promotional literature on the reward program can be very specific as to kinds of information wanted. Moreover, experienced intake analysts can readily discard paranoid ravings and idle speculation. The IRS has had no problem doing so in its long-existing program. Announcements of big rewards in cases of capital crimes always bring in a deluge of false leads, yet the police authorities regard the effort as worthwhile.

As for the problem of generating an atmosphere of pervasive suspicion, the fear is not grounded on any historical basis. Although the IRS does not publicize rewards, the program has been around so long that its existence is widely known. There is no perception that it has led to

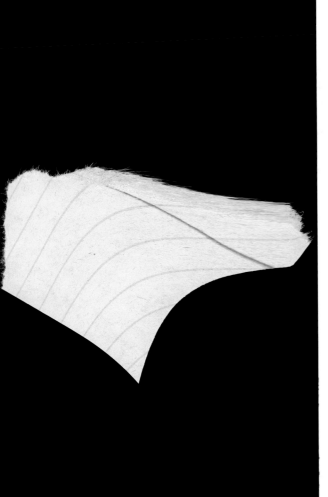

an epidemic of peddling neighborly confidences to the IRS. The point of publicizing the program is of course to encourage more tips and, if you like, more betrayal of confidential information, but there is no reason to believe that it will lead to an erosion of mutual trust beyond what has already occurred in modern American communities. (It might also lead to more discretion—less idle chattering and boastfulness about illegal corner cutting. It is amazing at times how freely people talk about working off the books or otherwise evading the scrutiny of the IRS.)

Society must own up to the realization that the informants' tips on which all police agencies are dependent, to some degree, are often volunteered for reasons that are less than noble and public-spirited. Without even being enticed by rewards, a disgruntled ex-employee turns in a former employer, someone in trouble with the law trades information for leniency, one competitor provides the authorities with damaging information about another, and so on. The motives may be base and self-serving, but the ends served—the ends of justice—are for once not befouled by the means.

By no means am I alone in this view. Congress, after all, did provide for rewards for information on insider trading. In 1986, it also passed amendments to the old False Claims Act that revivified the Civil War statute enacted during an earlier wave of concern about fraud by government contractors. The original act allowed private citizens to sue on behalf of the federal government and collect 10 percent of any recoveries. The ever-lengthening list of defense procurement scandals during the 1980s prompted the 1986 amendments, which raised the ceiling for rewards to 25 percent, required the Justice Department to decide within sixty days whether it wanted to join a private lawsuit, and allowed whistle-blowers who lost their jobs or were otherwise victimized to sue their employers for damages. If the government joins the suit, it runs it, with the private initiator remaining as coplaintiff. If the Justice Department turns it down, the private plaintiff can continue on his own, in which case his share of the proceeds, if he wins, can go up to 30 percent.

The legislation has become a very effective device to encourage whistle-blowers to come forward with inside information. From 1986 to early July 1992, the act resulted in the filing of 450 private suits. Most of them dealt with defense contractors, though the act applies to the entire field of government procurement. The Justice Department rejected 264 of the cases, joined in 81, settled 41 with payments totaling $264.2

million (none went to trial), and was still investigating the remainder.[7] The largest case accepted by the Justice Department was initiated with a complaint by a former Singer Co. employee named Christopher Urda of Binghamton, New York, who worked as a pricing administrator. He alleged that the company had fraudulently overcharged the Defense Department $77 million in billings for flight simulators during the 1980s. The case was settled late in July 1992, with the successor company to Singer agreeing to pay the government $55.9 million. The judge who accepted the settlement awarded Urda $7.5 million, the largest sum bestowed under the False Claims Act.[8]

With incentives of that sort in prospect, little wonder that the suits have come pouring in—but at a manageable rate; 450 over six years works out to a little more than one a week, which the Justice Department can handle. Understandably, defense contractors have been less than overjoyed at the refurbished law. Several have attacked its constitutionality, arguing that the plaintiffs lack "standing" in court because they cannot allege personal loss; the counter argument is that Congress can endow anyone with standing. So far, the lower courts have upheld the statute's constitutionality.

More aggressive use of tipster reward programs by no means exhausts the possibilities of government action. Both the FBI and the IRS conduct undercover operations, but other agencies that deal with business crime have no taste or training for them. Not that a lawyer from the antitrust division or the SEC would be expected to go undercover, or to direct an outside hireling who did so; the actual technical work would be in the hands of the FBI or the IRS. But the antitrust division or the SEC might sponsor such an effort when circumstances were suitable.

Some undercover operations place an agent in the middle of an ongoing conspiracy, and have the agent wired or in some cases videotaped to record incriminating statements or the actual passing of bribes. In other cases, a more elaborate sting operation is set up—a fictional conspiracy or a business—in which individuals with suspected predilections for the crime are invited to participate. (The classic one is to invite thieves to sell stolen merchandise to a fencing operation, which turns out to be staffed by a group of police.) More than a decade ago, the FBI ran what became the most celebrated sting in history—the Abscam operation—in which several congressmen and one senator were persuaded to meet with a phony Middle Eastern dignitary and offered bribes in return for legislative favors. They were convicted and compelled to quit Congress. In 1982, the FBI scored a similar success in California's Silicon Valley, nabbing representatives of two large Japanese electronics companies just as they were in the process of buying what they believed to be stolen IBM design plans from a dummy consulting firm set up by the FBI. The Japanese ultimately pled guilty and paid large fines.

A good example of what can be accomplished by an undercover effort was completed in New York in August 1987. A two-and-a-half-year campaign aimed at corrupt municipal officials in New York State, Operation Double Steel resulted in the indictment of fifty-seven persons in August 1987. It began with the U.S. attorney's office in Manhattan learning of an ongoing kickback scheme in which highway department officials around the state were bribed by vendors of snow removal equipment. The information came from some businessmen involved in the conspiracy who were caught in an unrelated delinquency and were trying to lighten their penalty.

The undercover assignment was handled by a single FBI agent who masqueraded as a salesman of snow removal equipment, employed by a company that had snitched to the U.S. attorney. The agent went about the state calling on highway superintendents who he had been told were on the take. He was provided with the code words to be used to indicate that a kickback was in the offing—something to the effect that the "usual commission" would be paid. Two schemes were involved (with the conversations being tape-recorded): the first a simple transaction in which the buyer placed an order and paid for it but no goods were shipped; in that case, the kickback was 50 percent. The other was a more conventional transaction, in which the items ordered were actually delivered and the kickback was only 10 percent.

There were a total of 105 instances in which kickbacks were offered, and in only one case was the offer rejected—on the grounds that it was too low, according to Rudolph W. Giuliani, then the U.S. attorney responsible for the case. In addition to nabbing forty-four individuals from forty communities around the state, the sting netted around a dozen persons who were vendors; they had hired the undercover operative as a representative after learning what an excellent selling job he had done. They put up some of the money for the kickbacks. All in all, it was a big catch for an investment that was not grandiose; its largest component was the agent's salary, plus traveling expenses and $40,000 contributed by the government as kickback money. Everyone was convicted, and the government recouped most of its money through fines.[9]

If the Justice Department can use an undercover agent to apprehend corrupt government officials, it can obviously employ the same technique in kickback cases in the business world or in defense-industry investigations when bribery of Pentagon officials is suspected. The use of an undercover agent often requires the cooperation of some legitimate business to provide cover, but not always. On occasion, the IRS gets a tip that someone is trying to sell a business and has been displaying or alluding to a second set of books. The service may then send around an agent, posing as a prospective buyer, to receive a compromising offer. But if it had the personnel, the agency could use the technique more frequently in pursuit of skimming cases—dispatching agents to retail establishments to work as waiters or salespeople. Undercover agents in securities firms might be useful to pick up leads about insider trading or stock price manipulation. If the antitrust division suspected price-fixing in a particular industry, it is not farfetched to suggest that a trained agent might be infiltrated into one of the companies involved to confirm suspicions and gather leads. The division could then proceed in the normal way by subpoenaing witnesses before a grand jury.

There are hazards in undercover operations, to be sure. Overzealous operatives can cross the line into entrapping suspects. Some agents may withstand the legal challenge of entrapment but still indulge in an aggressive and unfair degree of persuasion without which a crime might not have occurred. Cases of outright frame-ups have been known. All of which means that undercover operations have to be carefully monitored and controlled by a responsible enforcement agency. But the harvest of evidence and information that they bring makes them invaluable. Undercover operations have another advantage as well: if more were used, public awareness of them would eventually spread widely, and that in itself could become a deterrent. The tax-cheating owner of a fast-food joint might wonder if the new hire were an IRS agent.

Corporations also have a significant role to play in the campaign to repress business crime—a fact that is readily conceded but usually overlooked until a company gets into trouble. A good many companies, naturally, can hardly be expected to pitch in. A firm in New York's garment center caught in an invoice-purchasing scheme or some other tax fraud totally lacks the incentive—or the need—for a compliance program to persuade employees to obey the law, for it is the chief executive who decides to buy invoices and cheat on the company's taxes. Similarly, there is no need for a compliance program for top executives who authorize their employees to pay kickbacks to buyers. These chaps can only be restrained by the threat of being caught.

The situation is substantially different in large corporations, where the topmost rung of the executive ladder traditionally claims to have no acquaintance with the illegalities that may be found below. The decentralized management style in American corporations, with multiple profit centers, lends plausibility to the claim. Prosecutors cannot normally disprove it; otherwise they would have indicted the men at the top. It is not overly cynical, however, to suggest that many chief executive officers, having come up through the ranks, are reasonably well acquainted with what goes on below, without having knowledge of any specific offense. They are well endowed with what in Washington has become known as "deniability."

For example, how could anyone running an electrical contracting company not have known that bid rigging had been a venerable practice in the industry, any more than the chief executive or chief financial officer of a defense contractor would not have known that underbidding on a contract and then recouping through illegal overcharges was an all too common practice? To be fair, there may be some corporate chiefs—perhaps those who were recruited latterly at a high level or came up through the financial track while the hanky-panky occurred in manufacturing or marketing—who are honestly unaware of the pressures and delinquencies below and are as shocked as the public when a big case breaks. But it is hard to believe that there are many so ingenuous.

Once their company is caught, or a competitor is caught, many corporate leaders are suddenly persuaded that the short-term benefits of deniability are outweighed by the large financial penalties and blackening of the corporate name to which they are at risk if they do nothing. They decide to reform. Frequently, they have no choice. Settlements with the government, as in the case of the Sundstrand Corporation, often provide that the company introduce a satisfactory compliance program. Otherwise it is not allowed to bid on contracts.

The first requirement of a corporate cleanup program is resolve at the top. Not merely the promulgation of an elaborate code of ethics, training seminars, and signed statements of adherence to the code by

all managers, but in many cases an effort is required to transform the
mores, incentives, and managerial style that permeate the ranks and create an atmosphere in which illegality can flourish. Gary Edwards, the
director of the Ethics Resource Center of Washington, D.C., and one
of the most astute observers of the ethical dilemmas of business, makes
the point that one of the main problems is the common practice of management by objective. "In large organizations," says Edwards,

> sometimes the way we organize and manage causes certain mes-
> sages to be communicated that no one intends to communicate.
> When you rely heavily on management by objective, you feed
> a tendency to manage by the numbers. Most managers that I know
> have far more to do than they can get done. They live by trade
> off when it comes to performance evaluation. You focus on the
> guys who didn't get it all done. The guys who are meeting the
> sales quotas, you slap them on the back, and say do it again next
> quarter, and next quarter, of course, has to be better than the
> same quarter last year, and you end up sending a message in a
> company that management, top management, doesn't care how
> you get there, only whether you get there . . . and they plateau
> or move out people who don't get there . . . it's vicious, poten-
> tially and often in fact, and it's systemic . . . in every large com-
> pany that we've had anything to do with.

Management by objective is not in itself wrong, but it has to be leav-
ened with a concern for means as well as ends. Edwards points out that
"you could create an environment where people who can't get to the
objectives are allowed or encouraged to revisit them with their supervisors periodically." Beyond that, new norms of acceptable behavior have
to be established. Management must not only condemn explicitly the
commonplace illegalities formerly winked at but must be perceived as
aggressively seeking to ferret them out. The message must go out to all
ranks, as Edwards puts it, that "people get beaten into the ground if they
do the wrong thing."[10]

In recent years a growing number of companies, especially in the defense
industry, have established corporate ethics programs. An organization
called the Defense Industry Initiative on Business Ethics and Conduct
was set up in 1986 to encourage corporate self-policing and thereby ward

off more intrusive federal action; nearly fifty large defense contractors have signed up and regularly report on the progress of their efforts to the Washington coordinator of the group. The standard corporate compliance program consists of a code of ethics, indoctrination sessions for all hands, the establishment of a corporate compliance office with a full-time director, similar offices at division level, and the provision of telephone "hot lines" for queries, complaints, and allegations of misconduct.[11]

All these features are embodied in the ethics program developed at General Dynamics. The program began in mid-1985, as a result of a directive from Secretary of Navy John Lehman, who had suspended the contract bidding privileges of two of the company's divisions because of grievous cost overruns and other delinquencies, not least the expensive gifts it had been bestowing for years on Admiral Hyman Rickover, the father of the nuclear submarine and the patron of the corporation's Electric Boat Division. The establishment of an ethics program, with penalties for violations, was one of the requirements imposed by Lehman before he lifted the suspensions.

The company moved with dispatch, first arranging a daylong consulting session with Gary Edwards and other staffers of the Ethics Resources Center and then developing an elaborate program that many other companies have since come to regard as a model. The centerpiece of the effort is a detailed set of "Standards of Business Ethics and Conduct," neatly packaged in a slim, twenty-page pamphlet that is bestowed on every new employee, who has to sign a form certifying that the document has been read. The code covers every conceivable ethical misstep, in most cases providing a stern affirmation of what should be self-evident: gifts and gratuities can neither be given to customers nor accepted, "except for items that are clearly promotional in nature, mass produced, trivial in value and not intended to evoke any form of reciprocation"; bribes and kickbacks are forbidden; the antitrust laws are to be obeyed—no price-fixing or arrangements to allocate customers with competitors or agreements not to produce certain products; testing of products and documentation of the testing must be accurate; an investment by an employee in an outside supplier is undesirable (but may be approved by superiors in some circumstances). And much more.

A few of the points may not reek of the obvious, such as the injunction against business entertainment (including lunch), which would be an excessive restraint in most business relationships but is necessary to comply with Pentagon regulations. Yet even a catalog of rudimentary cautions may be useful in a document that seeks to lay down a code of conduct for every employee, especially the most untutored. It has the virtue of giving an explicit warning to everyone. When the General Dynamics ethics program was adopted, not only was it mandatory reading but all employees had to attend indoctrination lectures. The company also set up a corporationwide compliance effort, headed by a prestigious outsider— Kent Druyvestyn, a former dean at the University of Chicago School of Business—serving as ethics director at headquarters in St. Louis. Each of the company's thirty-two divisions and subsidiaries also appointed ethics directors, some of them full time.

The most useful of the program's innovations are the hot lines—twenty-eight of them throughout the company as of the summer of 1990. The telephone numbers are prominently advertised in company publications and phone books. All employes have a number to call; they can also telephone Druyvestyn in St. Louis over an 800 line. The virtue of the hot line, of course, is the anonymity it offers to anyone seeking an opinion on an ethical dilemma or wishing to alert the company to wrongdoing. Eighty percent of callers give their names, however, which is understandable because most calls are requests for information. Everyone is assured of confidentiality. Druyvestyn reports that the calls involve four main areas: conflicts of interest in relations with a customer; problems of allocating an employee's time between different customer's accounts, which seems to an outsider to be more of an accounting than an ethical problem; matters involving the private use of company property; and intramural relations between employees, such as charges of unfairness, harassment, racial discrimination. Allegations of wrongdoing by other employees and supervisors do enliven the hot lines, but whistle-blowers account for only a small volume of traffic. Other corporations have had the same experience. The hot line at Parker Hannifin, a manufacturing company headquartered in Cleveland, racked up 165 calls during the 12 months ending in June 1989; 113 of them involved personnel issues and only 14 dealt with security matters, a category that includes thefts and bribes.

General Dynamics publishes more statistics on its program than most companies. During 1986, ethics directors received 3,646 communications from employees by telephone, letter, and personal visit; the number rose to 5,482 in 1987, fell back to 5,379 in 1988, and to 4,955 in 1989—

variations that hardly seem significant. Each time a plausible report of wrongdoing was received an inquiry was launched; if the charges were sustained, sanctions would be imposed—from warning through reprimand to dismissal. (Accepting a minor gift would probably bring a reprimand; a kickback, dismissal.) As compared to the volume of communications, the number of sanctions resulting from ethics investigations appears to be modest: 123 in 1986; 205 in 1987; 206 in 1988; and 257 in 1989. For the year 1987, the company also published a breakdown of the sanctions: 139 warnings and reprimands, 29 suspensions, 27 discharges, 3 demotions, and 7 mandatory refunds for losses or damages.

What does all this prove about the program's effectiveness? Not very much. Druyvestyn measures effectiveness by the extent of employee awareness of the program; on this basis, he regards it as a success, for he says that companywide opinion surveys show universal awareness. But there are no data on how awareness affects behavior.[12] Companywide figures on sanctions, stretching back to the years before the program started, might show whether there has been an improvement in overall behavior. Or they might not because of laxness in past years; offenses might previously have gone undetected and unpunished.

While the General Dynamics program is fairly standard, some companies add other wrinkles. Hughes Aircraft has described a lot of computerized auditing to detect suspicious patterns in purchases that might indicate that buyers were corrupted by salespeople. Where possible, the company also rotated the assignments of buyers, to break up overly cordial relationships with sellers.[13] Other companies might usefully employ these techniques, though there is no absolutely certain way of avoiding the receipt of kickbacks. It should be easier to eliminate the giving of kickbacks, since they have to be financed in some covert fashion and most salesmen cannot do that on their own, unless the sums are modest enough to be concealed on their expense accounts.

If top management makes it clear that it means to crack down hard, it should be able to police its ranks effectively. One obvious technique, which no one seems to be in a rush to employ, is to make each level of supervision responsible for the delinquencies of subordinates—not in any legal sense but in terms of evaluating managerial skills and in apportioning penalties and rewards. That might not prevent the receipt of kickbacks, but it certainly could prevent tax fraud and procurement fraud, which unlike a kickback cannot be accomplished by an individual acting alone. The rogue manager of a unit might be kept from running amok if his boss knew that a scandal might threaten his own career.

With corporate crime, only scandal prompts reform or at least the semblance of reform. So far as one can see, there has been little spontaneous conversion of chief executive officers to the higher corporate ethics. In the end, any hope of significantly curbing corporate crime must start with the vigilance of the public authorities, who reveal the scandals. But vigilance can have only limited range with inadequate resources.

NOTES

Chapter 1

1. Source citations for the Sundstrand case will be found in the notes to Chapter 8, which discusses the case in greater detail.

2. Citations for the Levine, Boesky, and Siegel cases will be found in the notes to Chapter 5.

3. Citations for the Hertz case will be found in the notes to Chapter 7.

4. Citations for the invoice-selling (Gurary) case will be found in the notes to Chapter 6.

5. Adam Smith, *The Wealth of Nations* (Modern Library edition, New York: Random House, 1937), p. 128.

6. Edwin H. Sutherland, *White Collar Crime: The Uncut Version* (New Haven: Yale University Press, 1983), p. 7. This edition, with a useful introduction by Gilbert Geis and Colin Goff, contains the corporate names that Sutherland felt compelled to delete from the original edition.

7. Ibid., p. 15.

8. Marshall B. Clinard and Peter C. Yeager, *Corporate Crime* (New York: The Free Press, 1980), p. 16.

9. Ibid., p. 110.

10. Ibid., pp. 113–16.

11. Ibid., p. 122.

12. Irwin Ross, "How Lawless Are Big Companies?" *Fortune*, December 1, 1980, p. 5 et seq. Philip Mattera was the research associate for the article.

13. Office of Inspector General, Department of Defense, September 11, 1990.

14. Source citations are in the notes to Chapter 3, which has a full discussion of these cases.

Chapter 2

1. The brief synopsis here of the fight for control of the Erie is based in part on Matthew Josephson, *The Robber Barons*, repr. ed. (San Diego: Harcourt Brace Jovanovich, 1962), pp. 116–34; and Maury Klein, *The Life and Legend of Jay Gould* (Baltimore: Johns Hopkins University Press, 1986), pp. 79–86.

2. Josephson, *Robber Barons*, p. 123.

3. Roger Butterfield, *The American Past* (New York: Simon and Schuster, 1947), pp. 202–3.

4. Klein, *Life and Legend of Jay Gould*, pp. 99–115.

5. Samuel Eliot Morison, *The Oxford History of the American People* (New York: Oxford University Press, 1965), p. 732; Josephson, *Robber Barons*, pp. 351–58; Charles A. Beard and Mary R. Beard, *The Rise of American Civilization*, vol. 2 (New York: The Macmillan Company, 1943), pp. 307–11.

6. Beard and Beard, *Rise of American Civilization*, pp. 202–3; Josephson, *Robber Barons*, pp. 91–92 and 163–65.

7. Saul Engelbourg, *Power and Morality: American Business Ethics, 1840–1914* (Westport, Conn.: Greenwood Press, 1980), pp. 25–27; Josephson, *Robber Barons*, pp. 280–89.

8. Beard and Beard, *Rise of American Civilization*, pp. 182–91; Josephson, *Robber Barons*, pp. 115–20 and 277–80.

9. *United States v. E. C. Knight & Co.*, 156 U.S. 1 (1895); *Addyston Pipe and Steel Co. v. U.S.*, 85 Fed. 271 (6th Cir., 1898), modified and affirmed, 175 U.S. 211 (1899); Engelbourg, *Power and Morality*, pp. 109–10; Josephson, *Robber Barons*, pp. 381–83, 448–50.

10. Engelbourg, *Power and Morality*, Chapter 5, "The Moral Audit."

11. U.S. Congress, Senate, Committee on Banking and Currency, *Stock Exchange Practices*, 73d Cong., 2d sess., 1934, S.Rept. 1455, p. 126.

12. Ibid., pp. 133–50.

13. Ibid., pp. 30–38.

14. Ibid., p. 32.

15. Ibid.

16. Ibid., pp. 32–35.

17. Ibid., pp. 62–63.

18. Ferdinand Pecora, *Wall Street Under Oath* (New York: Simon and Schuster, 1939), pp. 150–51.

19. Ibid., pp. 153–61.

20. *Stock Exhange Practices*, pp. 63–66.

21. Ibid., p. 44.

22. A good exposition of the new legislation can be found in Sidney Robbins, *The Securities Markets: Operations and Issues* (New York: The Free Press, 1966), pp. 86–109.

Chapter 3

1. Robert H. Bork, *The Antitrust Paradox: A Policy at War with Itself* (New York: Basic Books, 1978); William E. Kovacic, "The Antitrust Paradox Revisited: Robert Bork and the Transformation of Modern Antitrust Policy," Washington Legal Foundation, Critical Legal Issues Working Paper Series no. 32, Washington, D.C., 1989.

2. News release from Department of Justice, Washington, D.C., November 19, 1990, "President Signs Bill Greatly Increasing Antitrust Penalties."

3. Herbert B. Newberg, *Newberg on Class Actions: A Manual for Group Litigation at Federal and State Levels*, 2d ed. (Colorado Springs, Colo.: Shepard's/McGraw-Hill, 1985), vol. 2, Sect. 11.02 for the settlement figures in the corrugated boxes, folding carton, and gypsum wallboard cases (the latter including interest). Settlement sums for the plywood, fine paper, and chlorine cases came from a leading plaintiffs' lawyer in these suits, Harold E. Kohn, of the Philadelphia firm of Kohn, Savett, Klein & Graf. (Letter of December 12, 1988 to author.)

4. Richard Austin Smith, "The Incredible Electrical Conspiracy," *Fortune*, April and May 1961, parts 1 and 2; John Herling, *The Great Price Conspiracy* (Washington, D.C.: Robert B. Luce, 1962); James Grant Fuller, *The Gentlemen Conspirators* (New York: Grove Press, 1962); Clarence C. Walton and Frederick W. Cleveland, Jr., *Corporations on Trial: The Electric Cases* (Belmont, Calif.: Wadsworth Publishing Co., 1964); Charles A. Bane, *The Electrical Equipment Conspiracies: The Treble Damage Actions* (New York: Federal Legal Publications, 1973).

5. Allan T. Demaree, "How Judgment Came for the Plumbing Conspirators," *Fortune*, December 1969.

6. I did not see the letter, but Antitrust Divison lawyer Hays Gorey, Jr., described it in some detail in an interview with the author on April 19, 1988. Andy Paszter, "Busting a Trust—Electrical Contractors Reel under Charges that They Rigged Bids," *Wall Street Journal*, November 29, 1985, deals with the letter in general terms, as well as with the ensuing investigation.

7. Telephone interviews with Jacquelyn Frend, Office of Operations, Antitrust Division, Department of Justice, December 20, 1990, and July 21, 1992.

8. Computer printout of electrical construction cases from Office of Operations, Antitrust Division, Department of Justice, April 18, 1988.

9. The foregoing five paragraphs derived principally from information provided by Gorey in interview, April 19, 1988.

10. Ibid.; *United States v. Fischbach and Moore, Inc., et al.*, Crim. No. 83–98 (W.D. Pa., Pittsburgh Div.). Before trial in February 1984, the Howard P. Foley Company pled guilty after a plea agreement and E. C. Ernst, Inc., pled nolo contendere. Tri-City Electric and James Oesterle were acquitted. Four individuals and three companies—Fischbach and Moore, Lord Electric, and Sargent—were convicted and lost on appeal. 750 F.2d 1183 (3d Cir., 1984). Cert. denied 105 S.Ct. 1397 (1985). Of the court documents, see the "Official Version of the Offense (Frederic B. Sargent)" and the government's sentencing recommendations for Fischbach and Moore, as well as the appellate opinion.

11. Interview with antitrust division lawyer David Jordan, July 11, 1989, in Washington, D.C. Court documents that provide useful details of the case, *United States v. Allegheny Bottling Co., et al.*, Crim. No. 87–123–N (E.D. Va., Norfolk Div.), include the indictment, opinion, and order (August 25, 1988) denying a new trial, sentencing opinion (August 30, 1988), and unpublished appellate opinion (No. 88-5147, 5th Cir., January 11, 1989). Cert. denied 110 S.Ct. 68 (October 2, 1989). For additional details on the origin of the case, see Michael P. Grim, "Uncapping a Conspiracy," *Virginia Business*, January 1989.

12. Telephone interview with Frend, July 21, 1992.

13. Interview with Gorey, April 21, 1988.

14. Telephone interview with Robert S. Bennett, September 17, 1990.

15. Jeffrey Sonnenfeld and Paul R. Lawrence, "Why Do Companies Succumb to Price Fixing?" *Harvard Business Review*, July–August 1978, pp. 145–57.

16. U.S. Congress, Senate, Judiciary Committee, Subcommittee on Antitrust and Monopoly, *Hearings on Administered Prices, Price-fixing and Bid-rigging in the Electrical Manufacturing Industry*, 87th Cong., 1st sess., 1961, p. 17294.

17. Ibid., p. 17403.

18. Ibid., p. 17296.

19. Ibid., p. 16736.

20. Office of Operations, Antitrust Division, Department of Justice, *Workload Statistics: FY 1980–1991*.

21. Staff figures from Thomas King, Executive Office, Antitrust Division, Justice Department, July 1992.

22. Spivack confirmed the quote to me in an interview in New York City, April 29, 1988.

Chapter 4

1. Much of the information on this case came from Fred D. Heather, the former assistant U.S. attorney in charge of it, whom I interviewed on March 8, 1988, in Los Angeles. The Bonner quote is from his statement before the Subcommittee on Oversight of Government Management of the U.S. Senate Committee on Governmental Affairs, in a hearing on February 27, 1986.

2. Sources on this case were Tom Bonner, Craig Brueckman, and Frank Crocco, agents of the Defense Criminal Investigative Service, who were interviewed on September 13, 1988, at their offices in Chester, Pennsylvania.

3. "Former Printer Pleads Guilty to Payoffs," *Chicago Tribune*, June 23, 1986.

4. Bonner, statement before Senate subcommittee, February 27, 1986.

5. *United States v. Juan Homs, Jr., et al.*, 73 Crim. No. 145 (S.D. N.Y.).

6. *United States v. Bethlehem Steel Corporation*, 80 Crim. No. 431 (RWS) (S.D. N.Y.). Of the various court documents, the government's sentencing memorandum gives the best account of the case's chronology; Arnold H. Lubash, "Guilty Plea in Shipyard Fraud," *New York Times*, August 8, 1980; "Bethlehem Steel Fined $325,000 in Bribery Case," *Wall Street Journal*, August 26, 1980.

7. Criminal informations, factual proffers, and plea agreements in *United States v. Richard R. Colino*, Crim. No. 87-305 (D.C.); *United States v. Charles C. Gerrell*, Crim. No. 87–304 (D.C.); *United States v. Serra*, Crim. No. 87–303 (D.C.); *United States v. Jose Luis Alegrett*, Crim. No. 88–0362 (D.C.); press release of U.S. attorney for the District of Columbia, July 14, 1987; articles on the Intelsat scandal in the *Washington Post* of November 25 and 26, December 1, 5, and 19, 1986; February 19, May 21, July 15, and November 16, 1987.

8. Apart from the interview with DCIS agents Bonner, Brueckman, and Crocco, the court documents in *United States v. Frank Coccia*, Crim. No. 87–00032–01 (E.D. Pa.), *United States v. Leo Lamar*, Crim. No. 87–00033 (E.D. Pa.), *United States v. Mario d'Antonio*, Crim. No. 87–00159 (E.D. Pa.) that were helpful included the indictments, plea bargaining agreements, and government's sentencing memorandums. See also "Pentagon Payoffs—Honored Employee Is a Key in Huge Fraud in Defense Purchasing," *Wall Street Journal*, March 2, 1988.

9. Interview with Heather, March 8, 1988; press releases from office of the U.S. attorney, Central District of California: "Ten Charged with Taking Kickbacks on Defense Contracts," April 24, 1985, and "20 Charged in Kickback Schemes on Defense Contracts," July 24, 1986; government sentencing memorandums in *United States of America v. Philip R. Kaiser, et al.*, Crim. No. 85–388–RMT (C.D. Ca.), and in *United States v. Ronald Emile Brousseau*, Crim. No. 85–387–JMI (C.D. Ca.), the latter containing the quotations from Brousseau.

10. Public Law 99–634, 99th Congress, approved November 7, 1986.

Chapter 5

1. SEC Litigation Release No. 11095 (May 12, 1986) dealing with its civil suit against Dennis Levine (86 Civ. No. 3726 [RO] S.D. N.Y.). Douglas Frantz, *Levine & Co.* (New York: Henry Holt, 1987), provides a slightly different calculation, showing that Levine grossed $13.6 million in insider-trading profits but lost $2 million, giving him a net profit of $11.6 million.

2. *SEC v. Ivan F. Boesky*, Litigation Release No. 11288 (November 14, 1986), 37 SEC Docket 78, and *In the Matter of Ivan F. Boesky*, Securities Exchange Act Release No. 23802 (November 14, 1986), 37 Docket 2.

3. *SEC v. Kidder, Peabody & Co., Inc.*, Litigation Release No. 11452 (June 4, 1987), 38 SEC Docket 914.

4. *SEC v. Drexel Burnham Lambert, Inc., Drexel Burnham Lambert Group Inc., et al.*, Litigation Release No. 12061 (April 13, 1989).

5. *In the Matter Of Ward La France Truck Corp.*, 13 SEC 373 (1943), as cited in Sidney Robbins, *The Security Markets* (New York: Free Press, 1966). Robbins has a useful discussion of the early cases, pp. 96–97.

6. *In the Matter of Cady, Roberts & Co.*, 40 SEC 907 (1961).

7. *SEC v. Texas Gulf Sulphur Co.*, 401 F.2d 833 (2d Cir., 1968).

8. *Chiarella v. United States*, 445 U.S. 222 (1980), reversing 588 F.2d 1358 (2d Cir., 1978).

9. *Dirks v. SEC*, 463 U.S. 646 (1983).

10. 16 Sec. Reg. & L. Rep. (BNA) 603, as cited and described by George Wang, "*Dirks v. Securities & Exchange Commission:* An Outsider's Guide to Insider Trading Liability under Rule 10b–5," *American Business Law Journal* 22 (Winter 1985).

11. *United States v. Carpenter, et al.*, 791 F.2d 1024 (2d Cir., 1986).

12. *United States v. Carpenter, et al.*, 484 U.S. 19 (1987).

13. John C. Coffee, Jr., "The Great Mail Fraud Flip-Flop: From Intangible Rights to Intangible Property," *White Collar Crime Reporter*, May 1988.

14. Interview with Joseph A. Grundfest on May 10, 1989, in Washington, D.C.

15. *United States v. Chestman*, 947 F.2d (2d Cir., 1991).

16. Interviews with John Sturc, then associate director of enforcement at the SEC, and with Richard V. Norell, a member of the enforcement staff, on June 7, 1989, in Washington, D.C.

17. *SEC v. W. Paul Thayer, et al.*, Civ. No. CA3–84–0471–R (N.D. Tex.); SEC Litigation Release No. 11923 (November 28, 1988); SEC Litigation Release No. 11992 (February 7, 1989).

18. *New York Times*, March 5, May 8 and 9, 1985; *Chicago Tribune*, May 9, 1985.

19. Among them SEC Litigation Release No. 11095 and 86 Civ. No. 3726 RO (S.D. N.Y.).

20. Ibid.

21. Interview with Gary Lynch on June 7, 1989, in Washington, D.C.

22. SEC Litigation Release No. 11288 (Nov. 14, 1986); *SEC v. Ivan F. Boesky*, 86 Civ. No. 8767 (S.D. N.Y.).

23. *SEC v. Kidder Peabody and Co., Inc.*, 87 Civ. No. 3869 (S.D. N.Y.). Litigation Release No. 11452 (June 4, 1987); *In the Matter of Kidder Peabody and Co., Inc.*, Securities Exchange Act Release No. 24543.

24. The government's June 15 sentencing memorandum in its case against Siegel, *United States v. Martin A. Siegel*, 87 Crim. No. 118 (RJW) (S.D. N.Y.), provides a concise and detailed account of Siegel's activities, his arrangements with Boesky, and the government's version of his relations with Freeman, Tabor, and Wigdon. Ironically, the memorandum provides details of his alleged swapping of information with Freeman (in instances apart from the single offense to which the latter pled guilty), which a different judge in the Freeman case refused to accept in the prosecutors' sentencing memorandum about Freeman. The newspapers printed the previously unavailable allegations. Freeman's lawyer was highly critical of the government, but to an outside observer the information does seem highly relevant to the Siegel case.

25. *SEC v. Drexel Burnham Lambert, Inc., et al.*, 88 Civ. No. 6209 (S.D. N.Y.); SEC Litigation Release No. 11859 (September 7, 1988).

26. Press release of Jan. 24, 1989, issued by the U.S. attorney for the Southern District of New York, together with plea agreement submitted to the court.

27. SEC Litigation Release No. 12061 (April 13, 1989).

28. *United States v. Michael R. Milken, et al.*, S 89 Crim. No. 0041 (S.D. N.Y.).

29. Press release of April 24, 1990, issued by the U.S. attorney for the Southern District of New York, together with plea agreement and criminal information to which Milken pled, *United States v. Michael R. Milken*, SS 89 Crim. No. 41 (S.D. N.Y.).

30. Lynch interview, June 7, 1989.

31. Telephone interview with Mary M. McCue, director, SEC's Office of Public Affairs, December 20, 1990.

Chapter 6

1. Among the court documents in *United States v. Prettyman*, Crim. No. 88–20 (D. Del.) that give a clear account of the case are the criminal information and the sentencing memorandums of the government

and defense. Tom McNichol, "The Seven Percent Solution," *Regardie's*, April 1989, provides some interesting details.

2. Internal Revenue Service, *Income Tax Compliance Research: Gross Tax Gap Estimates and Projections for 1973–1992*, Publication 7285, Internal Revenue Service, Washington, D.C., 20224, March 1988, pp. 3 and 5.

3. Ibid., p. 7.

4. Ibid., p. 3.

5. Internal Revenue Service, *Income Tax Compliance Research: Net Tax Gap and Remittance Gap Estimates* (Supplement to Publication 7285), Publication 1415, Internal Revenue Service, Washington, D.C., 20224, April 1990.

6. Internal Revenue Service, *Gross Tax Gap Estimates and Projections*, p. 3.

7. Ibid., pp. 13–16.

8. Ibid., pp. 4–8.

9. Ibid., p. 3.

10. Bureau of the Census *Statistical Abstract of the United States, 1989* (Washington, D.C.: Government Printing Office, 1990), table 1326, p. 753.

11. Interview with Bruce V. Milburn, then assistant IRS commissioner for criminal investigation, in Washington, D.C., September 20, 1989.

12. *United States v. Schnejer Zalman Gurary, et al.*, 86 Crim. No. 553 (S.D. N.Y.); 860 F.2d 521 (2d Cir., 1988); cert. denied, 109 S.Ct. 1931 (1989). Indictment, appellate briefs, and circuit court opinion provided the chronology, as did interviews with prosecutors Linda Imes, October 17, 1988, and David Spears, December 27, 1989, and January 5, 1990, in New York City. Lead defense counsel Nathan Lewin was also interviewed, on June 30, 1992, in Washington, D.C.

13. Walter Kiechel III, "The Crime at the Top in Fruehauf Corp.," *Fortune*, January 29, 1979, provides an excellent account of the case.

14. Milburn interview, September 20, 1989.

15. "Cartier and 2 Managers Indicted on Sales Tax," *New York Times*, March 20, 1985; "Furrier Is Guilty of Tax Evasion," *New York Times*, November 23, 1985; "Cartier Inc. Pleads Guilty in Sales-Tax Evasion Case," *New York Times*, January 29, 1986; "Bulgari Pleads Guilty in a Sales-Tax Scheme," *New York Times*, December 6, 1986; "Furrier Ordered to Pay $2 Million in Back Sales Taxes and Penalties," *New York Times*, June 10, 1987.

16. Statistical tables for "Returns filed, examination coverage and and results" from IRS annual reports.

17. Ibid.

18. "Highlights of FY 1991 Budget Request," fact sheet issued by IRS public affairs office, January 1990.

19. Telephone interviews with Wilson Fadely and Don Roberts of the IRS public affairs office, July 1992.

20. Unpublished IRS statistical table, September 1989, furnished by Fadely, plus additional statistics provided by him in June 1992.

21. *Rewards for Information Provided by Individuals to the Internal Revenue Service*, IRS publication 733.

22. Interview with Inar Morics, February 2, 1990, in Washington, D.C. (He succeeded Bruce Milburn as assistant IRS commissioner for criminal investigation.)

23. Ibid.

24. Hilary Stout, "The Real Loophole—Deep Problems at IRS Cause the U.S. to Miss Billions in Revenue," *Wall Street Journal*, January 2, 1989. Fadely confirmed that Goldberg had made the statement.

Chapter 7

1. U.S. Congress, House of Representatives, *E. F. Hutton Mail and Wire Fraud*, Report of the Subcommittee on Crime of the Committee on the Judiciary, 99th Cong., 2d sess., 1987, contains an exhaustive chronology of the case, together with the criminal information and plea agreement in the criminal case, *United States v. E. F. Hutton & Co., Inc.*, Crim. No. 85–00083 (M.D. Pa.), and relevant documents in the government suit for a permanent injunction.

2. *United States v. The Hertz Corporation*, 88 Crim. No. 462 (E.D. N.Y.); the criminal information provides useful detail, as does Hertz's stipulation and plea agreement. Interview with Assistant U.S. Attorney Jonny J. Frank, February 28, 1990, in Brooklyn, and telephone interview with William C. Harness of the Insurance Crime Prevention Institute, Westport, Connecticut, in March 1990. News articles in the *New York Times*, August 5 and 6, 1988.

3. Press release of the Department of Justice dated June 24, 1987, announcing the indictment of Chrysler (and two executives) and the

indictment itself, filed in the U.S. District Court in St. Louis. Andy Paszter and Amal Kumar Naj, "U.S. Charges Chrysler Altered Mileage on Cars," *Wall Street Journal*, June 25, 1987.

4. John Bussey, "Lee Iacocca Calls Odometer Policy 'Dumb'," *Wall Street Journal*, July 2, 1987.

5. Press release dated December 14, 1987, issued by the U.S. attorney for the Eastern District of Missouri, announcing Chrysler's agreement to plead nolo contendere and pay compensation. "Chrysler Finds a Way to Settle Odomoter Issue," *Wall Street Journal*, December 10, 1987; "Chrysler Pleads No Contest to Charges in Odometer Case, To Pay $16.4 Million," *Wall Street Journal*, December 15, 1987.

6. *United States v. Beech-Nut Nutrition Corporation, et al.*, 86 Crim. No. 715 (E.D. N.Y.); 871 F.2d 1181 (2d Cir., 1989). Interviews with two prosecutors in the case—John Fleder, director of the Office of Consumer Litigation of the Department of Justice, and Thomas Roche, executive assistant U.S. attorney (Eastern District of New York), were helpful in laying out the chronology, as was the indictment and the appellate opinion. Two magazine articles that appeared in the summer of 1988 had a wealth of detail: James Traub, "Into the Mouths of Babes," *New York Times Magazine*, July 24, 1988, and Tim O'Brien, "Bombs in Brooklyn," *The American Lawyer*, September 1988.

7. Traub, "Into the Mouths of Babes," p. 19.

Chapter 8

1. President's Commission on Defense Management, *Conduct and Accountability: A Report to the President* (Washington, D.C.: Ethics Resources Center, 1986).

2. Department of Defense Inspector General, *Semiannual Report to the Congress, Oct. 1, 1989, to March 31, 1990* (Washington, D.C.: DOD, 1990), chapter 3, p. 6.

3. *United States v. Teledyne Industries, Inc.*, Crim. No. 89–00007–A (E.D. Va., Alexandria Div.). See plea agreement and statement of facts, both documents filed with the clerk on March 23, 1989. In this jurisdiction prosecutors normally file statements of facts rather than sentencing memorandums.

4. *United States v. Loral Corporation*, Crim. No. 89–415–A (E.D.

Va., Alexandria Div.). Criminal information, plea agreement, and statement of facts were filed on December 8, 1989.

5. DOD Inspector General, *Semiannual Report, 1989 to 1990*, chapter 3, p. 8.

6. "A Guilty Plea by Emerson," *New York Times*, May 2, 1990; "Firm to Pay $14 Million Penalty," *Washington Post*, May 2, 1990.

7. "Maker of Aerospace Fasteners Pleads Guilty," *New York Times*, May 12, 1990.

8. "E-Systems Inc. Pleads Guilty to Fraud; Firm to Pay $4.6 Million," *Wall Street Journal*, August 29, 1990.

9. Ranking of defense contractors from the list "Top 200 Government Contractors," *Government Executive*, August 1990, pp. 13–16.

10. The thirteen corporations, alphabetically: Boeing, Emerson Electric, E-Systems, Fairchild Industries, General Electric, Grumman, ITT, Loral, Northrop, Raytheon, Rockwell International, Sundstrand, Teledyne.

11. Statistics from Bruce Drucker, director of the Office of Criminal Investigations Policy of DOD Inspector General, telephone interview, July 17, 1992.

12. I am indebted to Paul F. Math, the General Accounting Office's top expert on defense procurement, for digging out this figure, which cannot be found in the DOD section of the federal budget.

13. Office of Federal Procurement Policy Function, *FAC 84–5*, April 1, 1985.

14. Ibid., p. 16-2.

15. Ibid.

16. Clarence T. Kipps, Jr., and John Rice, *Living with Tina: A Practical Guide to the Truth in Negotiations Act* (Washington, D.C.: Washington Legal Foundation, 1989), provides a clear exposition and analysis of the act.

17. *United States v. Litton Systems, Inc.*, Crim. No. 86–00311–1 (E.D. Pa.); *United States v. Michael J. Millspaugh, Joseph DiLiberto*, Crim. Nos. 86–00311–2, 86–00311–3 (E.D. Pa.); *United States v. Roland Edward Fisher*, Crim. No. 87–246 (E.D. Pa.); unpublished opinion (No. 88–1174, 3d Cir., September 6, 1988). Indictments, plea agreements, government sentencing memorandums were helpful in providing chronology and details of the case, as was an interview with Robert I. Jacobs of DCIS on September 19, 1988, in Chester, Pennsylvania, supplemented with telephone interviews on April 5 and April 9, 1990, and a later interview on

August 7, 1992. "Litton to Pay $15 Million in Defense Fraud Case," *Washington Post*, July 16, 1986.

18. "Bell Copter and Army Settle Case," *New York Times*, March 11, 1988; "Bell Helicopter to Pay 80 Million to Settle Overcharge Allegations," Bureau of National Affairs, *Daily Report for Executives*, March 14, 1988.

19. *United States v. Sundstrand Corporation*, 88 Crim. No. 20021 (N.D. Ill., Western Div.). The criminal information, plea agreement, and government's "Offer of Factual Basis for Defendant's Pleas of Guilty" provide a wealth of detail on the case.

20. "Sundstrand to Plead," *Wall Street Journal*, October 13, 1988, third paragraph.

21. "Offer of Factual Basis for Defendant's Pleas of Guilty," p. 5.

22. "Auditor Asserts Contractor Tried to Impede His Search," *New York Times*, October 20, 1988.

23. "Contractor Disciplines 17," *New York Times*, January 7, 1989.

24. "Sundstrand's Head Retiring," *New York Times*, December 5, 1988.

25. Interview with Henry E. Hudson, June 27, 1990, in Alexandria, Virginia.

26. Ibid.

27. "FBI Tapped Phones in Pentagon Probe," *Washington Post*, June 16, 1988.

28. "U.S. Defense Consultant 'Steered' Jobs," *Wall Street Journal*, June 17, 1988.

29. Compilation of Operation Ill Wind cases dated June 2, 1992, issued by the office of U.S. attorney for the Eastern District of Virginia. See criminal information, plea agreement, and statement of facts in *U.S. v. Melvyn R. Paisley*, Crim. No. 91–00236 (E.D. Va., Alexandria Div.)

30. Compilation of Ill Wind cases dated June 2, 1992.

31. Ibid.

32. See note 4.

33. See note 3 for Teledyne. *United States v. Hazeltine*, Crim. No. 89–00006–A (E.D. Va., Alexandria Div.); *United States v. Whittaker Command and Control Systems*, Crim. No. 89–0320–A (E.D. Va., Alexandria Div.). Plea agreements outline the deals.

34. The U.S. government's "Offer of Proof" in the Hazeltine case gives a clear account of the complex case.

35. Compilation of Ill Wind cases dated June 2, 1992.

36. See note 5.

37. Telephone interview with Randy I. Bellows, assistant U.S. attorney in Hudson's office. These cases were all substantially the same. For details see, for example, the criminal information, plea agreement, and "Offer of Proof" in *United States v. The Boeing Company*, Crim. No. 89–00376–A (E.D. Va., Alexandria Div.).

Chapter 9

1. United States Sentencing Commission, *Sentencing Guidelines and Policy Statements* (Washington, D.C.: Superintendent of Documents, Government Printing Office, 1987).
2. Ibid., pp. 2.101–3.
3. Ibid., pp. 2.108–17.
4. Interview with Gary Lynch, June 7, 1989.
5. Staff and budget figures from Thomas King, Executive Office, Antitrust Division, Department of Justice.
6. Robert H. Bork, *The Antitrust Paradox: A Policy at War with Itself* (New York: Basic Books, 1978), p. 406.
7. Statistics from the civil division of the Justice Department, July 9 and 27, 1992.
8. Richard W. Stevenson, "A Whistle-Blower to Get $7.5 Million in Big Fraud Case," *New York Times*, July 15, 1992.
9. "Outline of Charges—Operation Double Steel," news release issued by office of U.S. attorney, Southern District of New York, August 11, 1987; interview with Rudolph W. Giuliani, November 7, 1988, in New York.
10. Interview with Gary Edwards, April 25, 1989, in Washington, D.C.
11. Interview with Alan R. Yuspeh, Washington coordinator of the group, June 28, 1990, in Washington, D.C.
12. Telephone interview with Kent Druyvestyn, director of the General Dynamics ethics program, at company headquarters in St. Louis on August 13, 1990. Pamphlets: "General Dynamics Standards of Business Ethics and Conduct" and "Ethics Program Update"; the latter contains the statistics. Parker Hannifin's ethics program report from Joseph D. Whiteman, general counsel, Cleveland, July 1990.
13. Interview with Dino Ruffini, staff vice president, Hughes Aircraft, March 14, 1988, in Los Angeles.

INDEX

ABOUT THE AUTHOR

Irwin Ross is a veteran journalist who has written widely on business subjects, crime, and politics. He is a longtime contributor to *Fortune*, a retired Roving Editor of the *Reader's Digest*, and the author of three previous books: *Strategy for Liberals*, *The Image Merchants*, and *The Loneliest Campaign: The Truman Victory of 1948*.